SPLENDORS OF MEIJI

MEIJI

TREASURES OF IMPERIAL JAPAN

MASTERPIECES FROM THE KHALILI COLLECTION

THE CURRICULUM GUIDE

FOR EDUCATORS AND DOCENTS

BY

DR. ROBERT STEVEN BIANCHI, PhD

BROUGHTON INTERNATIONAL PUBLICATIONS

Broughton International Inc. Publication
The Curriculum Guide For Educators and Docents
By Dr. Robert Steven Bianchi, PhD

ISBN 1-874780-18-8

Designed and produced by Martin Bragg Associates

Printed in China

Broughton International Inc.

James E. Broughton,
President

Dr. Robert Steven Bianchi
Director of Academic and Curatorial Affairs

TABLE OF CONTENTS

CHAPTER ONE

A BRIEF BACKGROUND TO JAPAN

Most of the objects featured in the special exhibition *Splendors of Meiji: Treasures of Imperial Japan* were made during the years between 1868 and 1912, a period of time referred to by the Japanese as the Meiji Era. Since the beginning of its written history, Japan has followed the traditional Chinese practice of numbering years, not as Westerners do from some fixed point in the past, but according to their order within eras of varying length. These eras are given lucky names such as "broad and eternal," "long-lived treasure," and so forth. The two Chinese characters with which the word *Meiji*, meaning "enlightened government," is composed were chosen with more care than usual, because the year 1868 marked a revolution in the way Japan was to be governed and heralded a half-century of change so profound that, as one historian has recently written, Japan "was not subjected to a long-term course of medical treatment, but rather underwent a major, and sudden, surgical operation."

This drastic medical intervention came about partly because of unresolved tensions within Japanese society and partly because of the growing commercial and military reach of Western nations. The relative importance of these two factors, and their respective contribution to the nature of the changes Japan underwent, are the subject of continuing scholarly debate. It remains a matter of historical fact, however, that it was not the older European powers but the youthful and expansionist American nation which made the decisive moves that were to force Japan into a new relationship with the rest of the world. Commodore Matthew Calbraith Perry's two visits to Japan in 1853 and 1854, conducted with a masterly combination of firmness and tact, set into motion a chain of events that would lead, within fourteen years, to the downfall of a system of government which was more than two centuries old, the reestablishment of the emperor as the symbolic, if not the actual, center of power, and the intensification of a process of reform that made one British scholar at the turn of the century comment:

> To have lived through the transition stage of modern Japan makes a
> man feel preternaturally old; for here he is in modern times—and yet
> he can himself distinctly remember the Middle Ages.

We shall be returning to Perry's visit below, but for our immediate purposes it is necessary to present brief sketches about the land of Japan and its features together with a synoptic history of this island-nation up to the moment of Perry's arrival. With this geographical, cultural, and historical introduction, one can better appreciate the background against which the art of the Meiji Era emerged.

GEOGRAPHY AND POPULATION

Japan is an island-nation occupying a vast archipelago of more than 6,800 islands. Yonaguni Island is roughly centered off the eastern coast of Taiwan, and Wakkanai on Hokkaido Island is about 150 miles further north than Vladivostok in the Russian Federation. If this archipelago, which hugs the coast of Asia in the form of a half moon, were to be superimposed over the East Coast of the United States, its northernmost frontiers would begin in Maine and its southernmost would reach into Florida, stretching over a distance of approximately 2,175 miles. The combined area of these islands is about 145,000 square miles, slightly larger than that of the state of California, but most of that area is occupied by Japan's four great islands, which north to south are: Hokkaido, Honshu, Shikoku, and Kyushu. Many of Japan's foremost cities are located on Honshu, including its capital Tokyo, as well as Yokohama, Kyoto, Osaka, Kobe, Nara, and Hiroshima. The country is divided into forty-seven prefectures for the purposes of its internal administration.

According to a recent census, Japan ranks as the eighth most populous nation on earth, with 126.1 million inhabitants. On average, there are approximately more than 337 individuals for each square half-mile of habitable land. Statistics suggest that 26.6 percent of this enormous population lives in Tokyo and the immediately surrounding prefectures. If one were to add together the population of just three of Japan's cities–Tokyo, Osaka, and Nagoya–one would find that their residents account for 43.6 percent of the entire population.

As an island-nation Japan is naturally surrounded by water. The Pacific Ocean forms Japan's eastern border, its northern frontiers face the Sea of Okhotsk, its western the Sea of Japan, and its south-western the East China Sea. These bodies of water wash over some of the four tectonic plates whose collision over the ages has altered the earth's crust via a series of warping and uplifting movements. This tectonic activity, together with that of volcanoes, has and continues to create the physical appearance of Japan. The intensity of the volcanoes, dozens of which are still active and even more of which presently lie dormant, is unrivaled in scale by any other volcanic zone on the earth. This volcanic activity–one-tenth of the world's known volcanoes are located in Japan–has created a great structural depression in the earth's surface called the Fossa Magna within which is Japan's tallest mountain, Fuji, a nearly perfectly formed geometric cone of ash rising majestically some 12,388 feet above sea level. There is such a complex framework of mountains in Japan as a result of this geo-logical activity that large expanses of somewhat level land developed only in certain areas of the islands and are restricted, for the most part, to the coastal plains. In fact, 68 percent of Japan is mountainous.

Tidal waves, termed *tsunami*, together with earthquakes are manifestations of the movement of the ocean beds as a result of tectonic shifting. That movement causes such great friction that the earth's crust melts, resulting in the formation of volcanoes spewing forth molten lava. As a result of this unceasing geological activity, Japan experiences up to one thousand earthquakes a year of varying magnitude on the Richter Scale, and the nation is dotted with geysers and hot springs, the latter often a source of recreational or therapeutic bathing.

THE SEA

In certain ways the sea has served as Japan's own natural wall, barring foreigners from interacting with her population. It was this barrier which was broken by Commodore Perry when he opened up Japan, an action which is described in greater detail below, and one which precipitated the events which led to the Meiji Restoration. The sea has also been Japan's most formidable ally, defeating invading forces in 1274 and again in 1281. In that year a flotilla, under the direction of the Mongol Khubilai Khan and consisting of 4,400 vessels and 140,000 men intent on invading Japan, did establish a beach-head, but a sudden typhoon, or *kamikaze* ["wind sent by the gods"] destroyed much of his fleet and impeded his army's withdrawal so much that half his fighting forces were lost in retreat. The significant role of the typhoon in that victory became so etched in the memory of the Japanese that the name *Kamikaze* was applied to the pilots of the suicide air attacks which characterized Japanese military strategy during World War II.

The nature of Japan as a nation consisting of almost 7,000 islands predetermines that few Japanese live far from the sea. As a result, the ocean has provided and continues to provide an economical means of transportation, and it has become the major highway over which much needed oil, ores, and foodstuffs have been imported into the island-nation. Furthermore, the fruit of the sea is a major component of the Japanese diet, particularly in the form of protein from the catches of tuna, salmon, and pollack. The meat of whales remains a delicacy. And the Japanese are wont to consume every denizen of the deep, boiling some up to extract protein which is then used in reconstituted food-stuffs or ground into fishmeal. Offshore fisheries have also been established at an exponential rate in Japan, and the sardine represents the lion's share of the crop which is then ground into meal and exported. The impact of the sea has led to an elaborate culinary ritual, if one can call it that, which involves the blowfish, called *fugu* in Japanese. Its liver in particular contains a toxin which can be introduced into the flesh of the *fugu* if not properly filleted, and is fatal to human beings when eaten raw, the preferable way to enjoy the delicate flavor of this and other fish. *Fugu* establishments display special designations and their chefs must be licensed. Still, deaths do occur, and tradition remembers a famous actor who became a victim of ill-prepared *fugu*, occasioning its chef to commit suicide immediately thereafter.

CLIMATE

The climate of Japan is characterized by humidity and seasonal changes not unlike those experienced by residents of the East Coast. The heat which characterizes Tokyo in summer should come as no surprise as that city's latitude coincides with that of the North African coast of Morocco and Algeria. Winter begins in late November and snow is not uncommon, particularly in the northerly parts of Honshu's "snow country." The deepest accumulation of snow ever recorded in Japan was almost 300 inches (more than 24 feet) in the Joetsu region of the southern Niigata Prefecture, while the coldest temperature, -41° C., was recorded at Asahikawa on Hokkaido, where winter temperatures average 8.5° C. Winter yields to spring in February, ushering in the pleasant month of April, when the northern passage of the *sakura zensen*, or cherry-blossom front, is loudly proclaimed by the media and inhabitants by the thousands flock to public parks, in theory to celebrate the arrival of spring and to appreciate the blossoms, but in practice to enjoy many pleasurable hours in the out-of-doors in a variety of celebratory modes. The first week of May, termed "golden week," because of the fortunate bundling of national holidays, such as *Kenpo kinen no hi*, "Constitution Day" (3 May), and *Kodomo no hi*, "Children's Day" (5 May), allows the inhabitants the chance to take extended vacations across the length and breadth of the country.

Toward the end of spring, temperatures and humidity rise ubiquitously across the islands, a harbinger of the arrival of the *baiu*, or early summer rainy season. As the *baiu zensen* clears the northern islands, it is replaced by a dominant south-easterly monsoon, which brings the islands hot days and sultry nights with very little relief in the way of breezes. Rain occurs as scattered thunderstorms, which can be torrential at times. The average temperatures in Tokyo and Osaka often exceed 25° C. in August, occasioning a series of local festivals in the northern part of the country which beckon thousands by promising an escape from the oppressive heat and humidity. By late August and September the front changes again, and Japan experiences its greatest amounts of annual rainfall during this, the *shurin* season, which is often accompanied by violent typhoons, an English word derived from the Japanese *taifu*, meaning "great wind." In contradistinction to the naming of hurricanes in America, Japanese number their typhoons in sequence annually, according to the order in which they are generated in the Pacific Ocean. It is only after a typhoon hits land and causes extensive damage that it is named, but such a name is given in retrospect, commemorating either the point of its landfall or the location of its greatest destruction.

Autumn in Japan is short-lived, arriving in October and lasting until the onset of winter in late November. The days alternate between sunshine and showers. As the temperatures begin to drop, the inhabitants flock to city parks and mountain valleys to catch the change of season as reflected in the brilliant transformation of the foliage.

These generalizations about the climate apply to all of Japan, but one must always be mindful of local variations effected by a number of climatological factors. The one glaring exception, however, is to be found in the southernmost regions of the Japanese archipelago among the Ryukyu Islands (including Okinawa) which, because of their latitude, enjoy a subtropical climate offering unique agricultural opportunities and facilities for tourism.

FLORA

Despite the abundance of rainfall, there are virtually no grasslands in Japan, the nature of the plains having been discussed above. The forests fall into three zones ranging from the subtropical in the south through the temperate to the boreal of the north. The types of trees growing in the former include evergreen oak, laurel, camphor, and camellia, while maple, birch, beech, oak, ash, chestnut, cypress, cedar, and fir dominate the flora of the temperate zones. In the boreal forests one can find birch, aspen, willow, and alder. Botanists estimate that there are between 4,000 and 6,000 native species of plants to be found in Japan. It is important to recall here that two-thirds of Japan's landmass is covered by forests, making Japan a world leader in the export of forest-related products. Nevertheless, these forests are not pristine, but represent either secondary growth which has been introduced as a result of an intensive use of the land or growth resulting from planned forestry planting. One can still find traces, however, of some of Japan's indigenous flora in areas not easily accessible, such as the higher mountains, the extreme northern limits of the country, or on some of the smaller, more remote islands.

Bamboo is to Japan what papyrus was to ancient Egypt, because of the variety of uses to which it is put. It can be eaten, or crafted into such diverse products as scaffolding, musical instruments, an assortment of kitchen utensils, brush handles, and vases. Known for its quick growth, bamboo makes an excellent ground cover, and tradition maintains that there is no safer place to be during an earthquake than in a bamboo grove because of its network of roots and runners.

Over time, the Japanese have developed their innate love of plants into unrivaled horticultural skills. Proof of that assertion is to be found, not only in the beautiful gardens which adorn shrines and temples nationwide, but also in their rock and moss gardens, and in the carefully manicured beds of irises and seemingly endless boulevards of cherry trees, especially when they are in bloom. Azaleas and tree peonies, the lotus, plum, and chrysanthemum (Japan's national flower which, when used as a motif on the art of the Meiji Era, sometimes signifies an imperial commission) are among the more popular flowers of the country. Because each of these have their own distinctive growing season, the Japanese are never at a want for beautiful flowers. The Japanese also excel in horticultural skills practiced on a more intimate, personal level, as seen in *ikebana* [flower arrangement] (discussed further in Chapter 2) and *bonsai*, the delicate art of miniaturization of nature's beauty.

Romantic images of floral Japan often include the traditional picture of tiny, irregular plots of rice fields, layered in terraces climbing up steep hills or creeping along the narrow floors of valleys. These farms are disappearing for several reasons, chief among which may be the push to convert such picturesque rice paddies into larger, more regularized, rectangular plots which facilitate all of the processes from sowing to harvesting. Like bamboo, rice has a multitude of uses in Japan which transcend its role as the staple of the Japanese diet. It is also fed to livestock and used to make *sake* [rice wine]. Its straw is manufactured into hats, sandals, and *tatami* [floor mats]. *Tatami*, rectangles generally measuring one yard by two yards, serve as modules in certain instances where, for example, the area of all of the rooms of a single house could be expressed in terms of the number of mats required to cover a given area. Special heavy ropes of rice straw are used to decorate the entrances of Shinto shrines.

FAUNA

As one might well imagine, a nation such as Japan with two-thirds of its landmass covered by forest is home to a number of sylvan beasts. Of these, 118 species have so far been identified. Although most are small rodents, bears, antelopes, and wild boar can be still be found in the more remote regions of the country. Deer, on the other hand, can be found not only in the wild, but even within the city limits of Nara and Miyajima, where special snacks are sold to tourists so that their children can feed them. The fox and *tanuki*, which resembles a badger and is often termed a "raccoon dog," can often be found near larger urban areas, and the Japanese macaque, or monkey, is common.

The Japanese raise both horses and cattle, and Japanese beef is known the world over for its tenderness as a result of its high degree of marbling. In order to produce such good beef, the cow is pampered to excess by a number of treatments which may include massaging with *sake*. In more recent years, Holstein breeds have been introduced for more traditional, Western dairy products.

The Japanese cat resembles the tailless British manx, while many dogs found in homes have dense coats and faces resembling huskies. Of particular note is the *Tosa*, a fighting dog of enormous stature. The district of Shikoku Island in which the *Tosa* was first bred is also famous for its ornate, long-tailed cockerels. During the Ice Age, because of the existence of a land bridge which connected Japan to Asia, mammoths and elephants roamed the northern and southern halves of Japan respectively. Japan also has its share of legendary, mythological beasts. The reptiles of Japan include sea turtles and sea snakes, and the giant salamanders of Kyushu and southern Honshu rank as the world's largest amphibians, attaining lengths in excess of three feet. Japan has two poisonous species of snakes, one of which is pickled in *sake* in order to produce a beverage noted for its stimulative qualities.

The avian kingdom is well represented in Japan by gulls and auks, as befits this island- nation, as well as by herons, ducks, geese, swans, eagles, kites, and pheasants. The crested ibis or *toki* has seen its numbers diminish in recent years, but not the crane, perhaps the best known of all Japan's birds. The cormorant still fishes, often for the delight of tourists.

Although Japanese life depends in many ways on the sea, its lakes and streams abound in trout, salmon, eels, and crayfish. The *koi* [carp], widely bred for exhibition and often seen in park and garden ponds, is also served up for dinner in expensive restaurants. Mosquitoes abound in summer as do crickets, the cicada, praying mantis, grasshoppers, and locusts, both of the latter still hunted in rice paddies by school children as an ingredient in a tasty snack. Butterflies are beautiful, and the members of the bright red and yellow *tonbo* [dragonfly] family can even be coaxed into perching on one's outstretched finger.

THE HOME

Housing in Japan has changed a great deal over the course of the last century, but traditional homes built of wood and clay with tiled roofs can still be found in the more rural areas of the country. The architectural styles of the vast majority of the homes in Japan today are modern, constructed primarily of steel, concrete, and wood. Because real estate is scarce in this populous country, particularly in the cities, houses and apartments are rather small by American standards and are proportionately more expensive. Because of the lack of space, urban dwellers generally entertain their guests in restaurants and perform the necessary ceremonies in community centers. In rural areas, houses tend to be larger and often include additional rooms for entertainment and the performance of ceremonies.

Because of the intense heat of the Japanese summer, homes are designed to permit the optimal passage of breezes through them. Rooms, therefore, generally have sliding doors and windows. The sliding doors and windows may be effectively used to reconfigure the views one has of the surroundings from the interior of the home. These architecturally sliding features have the added advantage of being removable so that two smaller rooms may be combined into one larger one. In a traditional home, the entrance or *genkan*, the corridors, and the kitchen have wooden floors, while the floors of the other rooms are lined with woven rice-straw mats, *tatami*. *Tatami* have been replaced in many modern Japanese homes by polished wood floors and carpeting, although *tatami* remains the floor covering of choice for bedrooms. Whenever one enters a Japanese home, whether family member or visitor, one removes shoes and dons slippers. The slippers are removed, however, before entering a room covered with *tatami* and are left in the corridor.

Some Japanese prefer to sleep on beds which resemble styles found in Western homes. Because of the limitations of space, however, other Japanese sleep on a *futon*, a soft, cotton-filled mattress. When not in use, the *futon* can be folded and stored in a special closet, sometimes after being aired out on a rack or balcony. This practice allows the space to be used as either a living or dining room during the day.

All homes have electricity and running water, but not central heating which is more common on Hokkaido because of its very cold winters. Elsewhere in Japan, heating is often achieved in the traditional way by means of a *kotatsu*, a low table that has a special electrical heating element built into its underside and is covered with a quilt. To stay warm, one can sit on a square, flat cushion, called a *zabuton*, with one's legs under the quilt of the *kotatsu*. Small electrical heaters and air conditioning units are also common.

The Japanese home has a special bathroom, the *furo*, which is used exclusively for bathing and is separate from the toilet. Its tub is rectangular, and filled with hot water. Before getting into the tub, one washes with soap and rinses off while sitting on a small stool. Once clean in this way, the individual can then enter the bath of clean, very hot water which produces a very relaxing effect on the body. As a result, the entire family can use the same tub of water without draining and refilling the bath with each use.

COOKING

Fresh ingredients are very important in traditional Japanese cooking. A typical dinner consists of rice, perhaps a soup, called *miso*, made from soybean paste, pickles, and either meat or fish. Popular seasonings include *shoyu* [soy sauce], *wasabi* [green horseradish], and *nori* [toasted seaweed]. Although rice is the main staple of the Japanese diet, fish is also an important food source. A favorite dish, *tenpura* [deep-fried seafood and vegetables] was introduced into Japan in the sixteenth century by Portuguese traders. *Sashimi*, thin strips of raw fish, and *sushi*, slices of raw fish on top of small portions of rice flavored with vinegar are other typical Japanese foods. Although *sashimi* and *sushi* may seem easy to prepare, it takes an individual many years to become an accomplished chef.

Red meat is not a traditional part of the Japanese diet, because of the natural scarcity of game animals and Buddhist taboos. The arrival of Europeans after the opening of Japan forced restaurants to cater to foreign tastes by initially serving *gyunabe*, a kind of beef stew. So controversial was this change of diet that a humorist of the period, Kanagaki Robun (1829–94) wrote a collection of satirical sketches on the subject, *Aguranabe* ["Eating Stew Cross-Legged"] in which a character concedes that an individual could not be considered to be civilized unless he ate beef. Over the course of the last century, however, new and delicious recipes have been developed for chicken, pork, and beef. *Yakitori*, grilled chicken on a wooden skewer, is popular along with *sukiyaki*, beef cooked in an iron skillet together with vegetables and *tofu* [bean curd]. *Sukiyaki* was, in fact, "invented" about this time as an inexpensive celebration of beef by students with limited budgets, despite the fact that the dish is now considered by many foreigners as a quintessential expression of Japanese cuisine.

Soba [buckwheat noodles] and *udon* [wheat noodles] are favorite substitutes for rice. These noodles are commonly served in a deep bowl of hot soup stock, topped with vegetables, fried bean curd, or *tenpura*. Cold noodles dipped in sauce make a refreshing summer lunch.

Cha or green tea is perhaps Japan's favorite beverage and is drunk hot, with nothing added to it. It is served after meals and whenever people get together. Other popular beverages include *kocha* [black tea], *sake*, and liquors made from malted rice and other grains or from fruits such as plums.

Lest one gain a false impression of the modern Japanese diet from these traditional dishes, one must remember that almost any food familiar to an American can be readily obtained in Japan. Fast food chains dot the landscape. People in Japan today enjoy omelettes, pasta, hot dogs, potato chips, yogurt, chocolate, ice cream, and cake; coffee, soda, and beer are common as well. Beer was introduced into Japan in 1868 from England and within a decade became extremely popular among members of Japan's administration and military.

FASHION AND CLOTHING

The traditional hairstyle of Japanese men with its focus on the topknot was replaced by more European-style haircuts when the members of the Japanese military first began to shave away their topknots in order to fit their heads into European-style military headgear. The Japanese also began to sport beards and moustaches at this time in imitation of their Western counterparts. A popularly sung ditty reflected this practice: "If you tap a cropped head, it will play the tune of enlightenment and civilization." By 1890, almost every male in Japan was sporting a European-style coiffure.

After the Meiji Restoration in 1868, the Japanese people began to abandon their native dress in favor of European and American fashions. Today, almost everyone wears Western clothing, from business suits to blue jeans. On special occasions, however, many women still like to wear the traditional *kimono*. It is worn wrapped around the body and tied with a wide sash, or *obi*. The *kimono* is commonly worn to celebrate the arrival of the New Year and to attend graduations. For weddings and other formal occasions, married women as well as their husbands wear a special black *kimono* bearing the family crest. Men may also elect to wear *hakama* [wide-legged trousers] and a *haori* [loose jacket] with their *kimono* on these occasions. Good silk *kimono* are very expensive, and many families maintain the tradition of handing them down through the generations. Because it is difficult to learn how to put on a *kimono* and its *obi* properly, many Japanese enroll in lessons for that purpose. Western-style shoes and socks are not worn with a *kimono*. Instead, either *geta* [high wooden clogs] or *zori*, low sandals made of cotton or leather, are donned. Special cotton socks or *tabi* are worn with these shoes, tailored with a slit between the big and second toe in order to enable the wearer to fit the toes around the sandal thong. A *yukata* is somewhat similar to a *kimono* but is primarily a simple, lightweight cotton robe which can be worn in the summer during festivals or when lounging around after a hot bath.

THE CURRENT IMPERIAL FAMILY

Under the constitution of Japan, the Emperor is the symbol of the State and of the unity of the people. He has no powers related to government. The Japanese imperial family dates back many centuries, as the brief history in Chapter 2 will reveal. Today, it represents the oldest unbroken dynasty anywhere in the world.

Emperor Akihito was born in Tokyo on December 23, 1933, the first son of Emperor Hirohito and Empress Nagako. While Crown Prince he married Shoda Michiko, now Empress Michiko, the eldest daughter of the former president of a major flour manufacturing company. Emperor Akihito acceded to the throne on January 7, 1989, upon the demise of his father. The imperial couple have three children. Crown Prince Naruhito (formerly known as Prince Hiro) is married to Owada Masako, the eldest daughter of Owada Hisashi, former vice-minister for foreign affairs. The second child, Prince Fumihito, married Kawashima Kiko, the eldest daughter of Kawashima Tatsuhiko, a professor at Gakushuin University. They have two daughters, the Princesses Mako and Kako. Emperor Akihito's third child is Princess Sayako who bears the title, Nori-no-Miya, Princess Nori.

Other members of the imperial family include Prince Hitachi, Emperor Akihito's younger brother, who is married to Princess Hanako; Princess Takamatsu; Prince and Princess Mikasa; Prince and Princess Tomohito of Mikasa; Prince Katsura; and Prince and Princess Takamado. The last named three princes are sons of Prince Mikasa, who is the younger brother of the late Emperor Hirohito.

CHAPTER TWO

A BRIEF HISTORY OF JAPAN

PALEOLITHIC PERIOD (50,000–10,000/8,000 B.C.)

The proven existence of a land bridge connecting Japan and Asia during the period from about 1,000,000 to 10,000 B.C. suggests that the earliest inhabitants of Japan were immigrants from mainland Asia who arrived on foot. The Asian origin of the Japanese appears to be confirmed linguistically because the Japanese language has affinities with both the Korean and Ural-Altaic tongues of northern Asia. On the other hand, several major Japanese myths, seen against the background of specific Japanese customs and architectural styles, argue in favor of a Polynesian and/or South-East Asian origin for these early immigrants. The conflicting nature of the evidence compels most scholars to accept that these earliest inhabitants may have come from several different regions.

By 50,000 B.C during the Paleolithic Period, or Old Stone Age, the inhabitants used a variety of stone tools to support themselves as hunter-gatherers. There is no evidence to suggest that they developed the craft of pottery-making. Although they were primarily nomadic, at least thirty different sites datable to this period have been identified which are characterized by dwellings and hearths, suggesting a more sedentary lifestyle for at least some of these people.

JOMON PERIOD (10,000/8,000–300 B.C.)

During the Neolithic Period, or New Stone Age, around 8,000 B.C., the archeological record reflects a major change in the material culture of the archipelago. It is moot whether or not these changes occurred within Japan as its society developed or whether they were either imported from abroad or introduced by newly arrived immigrants. On the basis of cultural analogies, however, one would be more inclined to regard these developments as indigenous, perhaps as native responses to foreign catalysts. It must be noted, nevertheless, that most of the sites from this period are localized in the northeastern part of the archipelago, which is furthest away from the Asian continent.

The stone tools reflect technological developments not only in the quality of their manufacture but also in the range of new types which seem to have been introduced at this time. These include axes and knives as well as fish hooks, with which the inhabitants of Neolithic Japan distinguished themselves as excellent hunters and fisherman. Deer and boar were a staple of their diet, as was shellfish. Excavated refuse dumps, termed kitchen middens by archeologists, reveal a fondness for seafood in the form of the discarded sea shells, thereby establishing Japan's dependency upon the sea as a source of protein at a very early date. Although not farmers in the true sense of the word, these Neolithic inhabitants seem to have grown nuts and berries, and seem to have adopted a more sedentary way of life as well. They lived initially in caves, but gradually developed a characteristic dwelling, the *tateana*, a circular pit-dwelling, the ceiling or roof of which was covered with thatch. Excavated examples are almost uniformly two feet deep and fifteen feet in diameter, creating an ample area in which a family of four to five could comfortably reside. The regularity of the *tateana* calls to mind the later modular use of *tatami* for defining areas within certain types of Japanese dwellings.

By 8,000 B.C. these inhabitants were creating the world's oldest examples of pottery. Created by hand without the use of a potter's wheel, these vessels exhibit a wide variety of shapes, perhaps indicative of local taste. Nevertheless, most examples are decorated with rope-like patterns, termed *jomon* in Japanese, which have given their name to Japan's Neolithic Period. The introduction of Jomon pottery heralds an interest in the craft of ceramics in which the Japanese were to continue to excel for thousands of years.

The Neolithic Japanese also created the archipelago's earliest sculpture, nowadays termed *dogu*, all of which are made of clay and can be conveniently divided into different types. One group represents fabulous composite beasts combining human and animal forms. Another type depicts "pregnant" female figures reminiscent of the fertility figures of contemporary Neolithic Eurasian cultures. Some *dogu* were apparently made in order to be damaged because examples exist in which the limbs of the figures appear to have been deliberately destroyed. The reasons for such ritual mutilations are difficult to discern, but some have suggested the practice was medical in nature, perhaps to alleviate ailments which afflicted arms and legs. This ritual practice was concurrent with a nascent belief in an afterlife. The Neolithic inhabitants of Japan interred their deceased, in the fetal position, in crude holes in the ground.

One of the most salient characteristics of Jomon-Period Japan, however, is revealed by a study of its material remains as well as its dwellings and pit graves–it appears to be a classless society. Dwellings and pit graves are of uniform size, and no set of objects appears to be any more numerous or luxurious than any other. This distinct absence of a spectrum of differentiation suggests a non-stratified social organization with no perceptible hierarchy based on material wealth. Towards the end of the Jomon Period, peoples from southern China and northeastern Asia, the first of several waves of immigrants who continued to arrive until about A.D. 500, entered Japan by way of Korea. These immigrants changed the face of the archipelago by introducing the cultivation of rice.

YAYOI PERIOD (300 B.C.–A.D. 300)

With the arrival of these new immigrants, Japan was transformed into a fully agricultural society with its own class distinctions and social hierarchies. These may have developed as a result of the introduction of rice whose cultivation in Japan was nurtured by alluvial wetlands which provided a perfect microclimate. The growing of rice fostered the development of permanent farming communities whose members were soon to be differentiated into social classes of unequal status. The immense expenditures of physical labor which rice cultivation demanded gave rise to two tightly organized local groups: family and village. The importance of rice to Japan cannot be understated, and in time rice became the main staple of the archipelago's economy. Other grains such as millet, wheat, and barley, also introduced from Asia, began to be grown on the mountainsides. This agricultural revolution was quickened by technological advances in the smelting of ores, likewise introduced by the newly arrived immigrants. These metals, iron and bronze, were primarily imported from the Korean Peninsula. Iron arrived either as ore or in the form of ingots which could then be smelted and crafted in workshops. Bronze was principally imported as finished products, some of them destined to be melted down and recast.

The classless society of the Jomon Period was now transformed as local and regional hierarchies developed. The newly introduced metals contributed to increasing social distinctions as well: the unequal distribution of ceremonial objects such as bronze bells reveal the existence of social stratification, as do the practical purposes to which iron was put. Unlike bronze, iron was primarily crafted into tools and implements, foremost of which was the forging of weapons. With such enhanced weaponry, individuals possessed the potential for consolidating ever larger territorial units into their emerging domains. Military and administrative hierarchies were a natural result, but distinctions also emerged in other cultural arenas, including burial customs. So, for example, in Kyushu, the deceased were interred in large urns or stone cists, sometimes clustered together in the necropolis under dolmens. In Kyoto and Nara, on the other hand, individual families appear to have owned specific plots of land within cemeteries and separated these real estate holdings from those of their neighbors by a series of trenches. Within these familial plots, wooden coffins were the norm for adults and pottery vases for children.

The rope-decorated handmade pottery of the Jomon Period was superseded in the Yayoi Period by elegant pottery thrown on a wheel, the aesthetic of which relied on its profile and shape rather than on its decoration. In fact, very often pottery of the Yayoi Period eschews all forms of decorative adornment.

Contacts with the Asian continent continued to increase during the Yayoi Period. Toward its close, the inhabitants of northern Kyushu became incorporated into the tributary system of China's Han and Wei Dynasties. A seal found accidentally by farmers in 1784 in northern Kyushu is thought by many reputable scholars to be the authentic seal given by Emperor Guangwu of the Chinese Han Dynasty in A.D. 57 to the legates from a district of the archipelago by which their land was invested as a tribute-bearing state. Such dependencies were further emphasized by the appearance of luxury goods of Chinese manufacture imported into the archipelago and by documentation in the annals of Chinese court ethnographers. Their records contain priceless descriptions of the Japanese inhabitants during this period before the development of writing in Japan.

These Chinese chroniclers called Japan the land of Wa, writing that designation with a character that means "dwarfed" or "stunted." They further described that land as consisting of a hundred, perhaps to be taken metaphorically as "many," tribes, reflecting no doubt the archipelago's regional differences seen, for example, in the differing funereal practices described above. Toward the close of the Yayoi Period, these same Chinese chroniclers reported that the civil disorders in Wa were put to an end when a queen named either Himiko or Pimiko consolidated her political position and established her hegemony over a wide geographic area. Because of the difficulties in correlating the geographic descriptions of these annals with the topography of the archipelago, the location and extent of Himiko's domain, which is there recorded as Yamatai, remains speculative, but almost certainly included northern Kyushu. She is reported to have based her authority on magic and sorcery. In this regard, the person of Himiko conforms to one of the characteristics of later sovereigns of Japan who were mandated to serve as mediators in a shamanistic sense between their subjects and the gods, a function which was regarded as the most sacred of the sovereign's obligations. This information about early religion in Japan, gleaned from descriptions of Wa preserved in Chinese dynastic histories, seems to allude to very early forms of belief systems which collectively came to be known as Shinto.

Shinto

In describing early religious practices and beliefs in Wa, the Chinese chroniclers remarked that they were wont to clap their hands in worshipping and that they placed great value in ritual purification. Although the deities associated with the clapping and the benefits derived from ceremonial ablutions have neither been clearly identified nor closely defined, it seems clear that Shinto, literally "the way of the *kami*," has very ancient origins. Although the word *kami*, which has connotative meanings of "above" and "upper," is often translated into English by the word "gods," its denotative meaning is far deeper. One turns, therefore, to a classic definition of *kami* adduced by Motoori Norinaga (1730–1801), a noted scholar committed to revitalizing Shinto. The word *kami* refers, in the most general sense, to all divine beings of heaven and earth that appear in the classics. More particularly, the *kami* are the spirits that abide in and are worshipped at the shrines. In principle human beings, birds, animals, trees, plants, mountains, oceans, all may be *kami*. According to ancient usage, whatever seemed strikingly impressive, possessed of the quality of excellence, or inspired a feeling of awe was called *kami*. *Kami*, therefore, encompass a polytheistic host whose members, like those of other very ancient animistic belief systems, inhabit nature on every level. *Kami* are consequently associated with life as a universally vital, creative force. The *kami* are intimately associated with human beings and with their most basic, if not the oldest, form of social organization, the family and its kinfolk in the rural farming community.

Shinto is a religion rich in myths and legends. The creation myth has parallels elsewhere, and may in fact be indebted to or colored by Chinese cosmology. According to the Shinto version, the beginning of the world, originally in a state of chaos, gradually formed as lighter particles of matter rose and heavier ones sunk, forming heaven and a kind of viscous ocean or sea. *Kami* then materialized and after seven generations had passed, Izanagi and Izanami, brother and sister, were commanded to create a "drifting land," and did so when Izanagi withdrew his spear from the ocean floor and the liquid dripping from its tip formed a small island. By means of a miraculous bridge, the siblings crossed over to the newly created island and there begot not only the rest of the islands which comprise Japan's archipelago, but myriad deities as well.

Izanami was so badly burned giving birth to the fire deity that she was forced to descend into the netherworld. Izanagi, in his zeal to recover his sister and bring her back to the world of the living, followed her but found Izanami's body so decayed and maggot-infested that he abandoned his resolve and retreated. Requiring purification in good Shinto tradition, Izanagi cleansed himself in a stream, and immediately created a new host of *kami*. The sun goddess, Amaterasu, was created as he washed his left eye and her brother, the storm god, Susano-o, appeared from his left nostril. Legends concerning both of these Shinto deities are depicted on objects on view in this exhibition, two episodes of which are discussed below.

Other episodes of Shinto myth deal with the hostile interaction of Amaterasu and Susano-o, and involve Amaterasu's appointment as ruler over the lofty celestial plateau, an act which insured her unassailable preeminent position within the Shinto pantheon, and caused her to be regarded subsequently as the ancestor of Japan's emperors. Susano-o, her brother, who possessed a somewhat sadistic character, was given the sea as his domain. Before assuming this role, he insisted on visiting his sister to bid her farewell. Susano-o, however, so tormented his sister by committing a series of unspeakable outrages against her that the frightened Amaterasu withdrew to a cave, thereby plunging the world into darkness. In order to lure her out of her self-imposed exile and restore light to the world, other *kami* in heaven resolved to participate in a raucous festival, the beginning of which was to be announced by a cockerel set atop a *torii* [arch]. Her curiosity thereby aroused, Amaterasu made her way to the cave's mouth, whereupon a muscular *kami*, seizing her, pulled her into the open and restored sunlight to the world. Some associate the *torii* of this story with the *torii* which habitually serve as entrance ways to Shinto shrines to this day. In fact, many Shinto shrines in remote areas are nothing more than a *torii*.

These myths of Shinto speak volumes about its tenets. The abhorrence experienced by Izanagi as he beheld the decomposing body of his sister Izanami in the hereafter reveals how the principles of Shinto are distanced from death. Indeed, Shinto developed neither a compelling eschatology nor any other vehicle by which the concept of life after death was presented. The concept of separating the good from the evil on the basis of deeds performed in life and of rewarding the former and eternally punishing the latter is completely lacking in the doctrines of Shinto. Dead spirits, regardless of their moral character, are consigned to the same fate, often, although not invariably, congregating upon the summits of holy mountains, prominent among which is Fuji. From there, some maintain, the spirits may, upon receiving ritual attention at specified times, return to bless their living family members. From this vantage, one may fairly state that Shinto is exclusively preoccupied with life in this world. Nevertheless it would be too facile, and grossly misleading, to suggest that the Japanese are Shinto in life and Buddhist in death. That said, it must be noted that Shinto does not possess a significant corpus of commandments regulating human intercourse on a moral and ethical level, in contradistinction to Confucianism (discussed later in this chapter). This, of course, does not mean that Shinto condones anti-social behavior. Such behavior is often associated with the upsetting of nature's harmony in the form, for example, of natural disasters. Special rites, principle among which are purification and exorcism, are then performed in an attempt to redress the imbalance.

Nevertheless Shinto does place a great deal of importance on *makoto*, "sincerity," and that principle has always been a moderating influence on Japanese society throughout the ages. The connotations of *makoto* are not easily communicated to an Occidental audience, but are linked to human emotions in such a way that one's feelings and actions must adhere to this principle of sincerity. This "ethic of the emotions," as one scholar termed it, remains the dominant feature of Shinto-based social intercourse and takes precedence over the other moral values such as good and truth.

Although most *kami* are benign, *tatarigami*, "malevolent spirits," do exist and must be propitiated as required. Some historians of religion would argue that *tatarigami* were not initially integral to Shinto, but were amalgamated into that belief system, perhaps even at a very early time, as a result of influences from the Asian continent. These same historians are in agreement as well that another feature of Shinto, shamanism, is also of foreign origin. Japanese religious history is filled with episodes about shamans and their ability to neutralize *tatarigami*. These individuals are more often than not women who are capable of entering *kamigakari*, "*kami* possession," or an ecstatic state which enables the malevolent deity to enter her body in order to reveal the nature of its displeasure and proscribe the steps necessary to appease it.

The purification rituals associated with Shinto divide into two, *kessai* and *harai*. *Kessai* deals with physical, external purification of the type commonly performed by a worshipper in a Shinto shrine, who simply accomplishes the ceremony by the symbolic rinsing of hand and mouth with water. *Harai*, or internal purification associated with exorcism, may only be performed by a priest employing a waving wand during the course of the rite, after which the previously possessed individual's spirit is restored to its flawless, pristine state.

One of the most enduring and colorful features of Shinto is the practice of *matsuri*, "the festival," when a *kami*, symbolically represented by either an emblem or other suitable object, is carried about the countryside in a portable shrine borne on the shoulders of young men. Such festivals are the occasion for merry-making and the consumption of quantities of *sake*.

KOFUN PERIOD (300–710)

As in the discussions of the earlier periods, those factors which contributed to the transformation of the archipelago from the Yayoi to the Kofun Period are difficult to define, although some have argued that the change was due to an invasion by horse-riding peoples from abroad. Whatever the agents of the transformation may have been, this new period inaugurates the era of the imperial dynasties in Japan, which some regard as the successor kingdoms to Himiko's Yamatai. The change of culture and the emergence of the Yamato State are made manifest by the stone and earthen burial mounds, called *kofun*, in which the monarchs of the period are buried and from which the name of this epoch of Japan's history is named. Some of these burial mounds are efficiently reworked hills or knolls, converted into tombs, but others are of extraordinary size which must have required an extensive expenditures of time, labor, and resources, and are assumed on that basis alone to be the final resting places of some of these early emperors of Japan. One of the largest *kofun*, which measures more than 1,500 feet in length, is in the outskirts of Osaka. It is said to be the resting-place of Emperor Nintoku.

The most salient external feature of the *kofun* is its decoration. In the early years of this period, that decoration took the form of plain cylinders, the purpose of which is debated. Some scholars have argued that such cylinders were functional, placed at strategic locations on the *kofun* to retard erosion. Others argue for their sacral function, suggesting they served as sacred markers to delineate areas of the *kofun* for ritual purposes. In time these cylinders were replaced by *haniwa*, terracotta statues, several feet in height, which represent a range of subjects from human beings, animals, houses, and boats. Whether the earlier simple cylinders were the linear, artistic ancestors of the later *haniwa* remains moot, but *haniwa* have been convincingly defined as reproductions of familiar images from life on earth for the emperor's afterlife. Removed from their context, the *haniwa* exhibit neither decoration nor attributes which connote a religious function.

Just as the *haniwa* replaced the cylinders, so too did the complex of funereal goods interred within the *kofun* change over time. In earlier *kofun*, archeologists discovered objects mostly in bronze with purely ornamental or ritual functions. In *kofun* dating from the early fifth century, those objects were partially replaced by others of a more practical nature such as iron tools and weapons. Many of these objects are thought to have been crafted in Japan by Korean immigrant artisans. The new focus on practical, iron goods within the *kofun* corresponds with the themes of the *haniwa* without, which now depict warriors and their mounts. The themes of these *haniwa* provide the evidence used by some in arguing for the period's origin. Whatever those origins may have been, there can be no doubt about the military character of the Kofun Period. This is clear not only from the *haniwa* and objects associated with its later mound burials, but also from the period's documented policy of expansion into the Korean Peninsula which may have resulted in the establishment of a Japanese presence at Mimana, defined by some scholars as a Japanese military colony but by other scholars, particularly those in Korea, as an outpost of the Korean Paekche Kingdom manned by the forces of Yamato. During the fifth century, Japanese involvement in Korea is also reflected in a succession of diplomatic requests to China, the objective of which was the confirmation of titles on Japanese leaders indicative of their military domination of parts of the Korean Peninsula. It was during this same century that scribes from the Korean state of Paekche introduced the Chinese system of writing which was adopted by the Yamato Court of Japan. From 507 onwards Japanese aristocratic families were encouraged to chronicle their histories.

Japanese writing

The affinities which the Japanese language shares with its neighbors has already been discussed in this chapter. Here the focus is on the writing of the language which has been characterized by serious linguists as the most cumbersome and complex notational system ever devised by any culture on earth. Some would even go so far as to call this system bizarre. The reason for such characterizations are readily grasped. Modern Japanese is written with a combination of four different systems: romanization which incorporates both Arabic and Roman numerals and the writing of certain words, notably proper names found in advertising and trade marks, in the letters of their original language; two syllabaries of over forty symbols each, *hiragana* and *katakana*, the former primarily used to write grammatical elements such as particles and suffixes, the latter nowadays principally reserved for loan words other than Chinese; and finally several thousand *kanji*, the Chinese characters themselves which were adopted by the Yamato Court. All four systems can be found together in one and the same newspaper article, for example, very often exhibiting two different orientations.

In trying to render words written in this complex notational system into English, one of two methods is traditionally employed. The first was developed by an American missionary, James Curtis Hepburn, who compiled a Japanese-English glossary published in 1867. The Hepburn system enables an English speaker to pronounce Japanese with reasonable fidelity with minimal effort. The *kunreishiki*, or official instruction system, introduced by the Japanese government in 1937, is more accurate in reproducing the fundamental structure of the language's vocalization but is little used today. Both systems, each possessed of ardent advocates, have their advantages, but the differences between them are, in actual practice, slight.

Social order

Over the course of time, the rulers of the Yamato State revamped the administration of their realm by gradually replacing bonds of fealty and allegiance with a fixed, regulated system of social organization. These initial administrative measures at clearly defining one's role in society were systematized in the seventh century by the Taika Reform which adapted certain bureaucratic mechanisms of China's Tang Dynasty to enhance the power and authority of Japan's central authority. That Japan should model its organizational structures on that of China should come as no surprise when one stops to consider that Tang-Dynasty China was in fact the largest and most powerful political entity in the world. To that end, a provincial administrative system was introduced as was a population census and a system of taxation of individuals on the basis of crop yield. In order for this system to work, the government relied on an army of bureaucrats whose salaries it paid.

The emperors of Japan are thought to be descended from the ruling family of the Yamato State which was formed at this time in the Yamato region of Japan, near present-day Kyoto and Osaka. These rulers worshipped Amaterasu and other deities associated with the native religion that later came to be called Shinto, discussed under its own heading above. An exemplar of that dynasty and of the reforms of the Yamoto State can be found in the person and career of Shotoku Taishi (574–622), who did much to enhance the power and prestige of Japan's central government, the capital of which was later at Fujiwara at the mouth of the Asuka Valley. He created a merit system of twelve ranks into which courtiers were enrolled on the basis of achievement rather than birth, and followed that with a seventeen-point "constitution," the provisions of which sought to regulate the ethical conduct of high ranking courtiers by laws linked to Confucian ideals. He fostered the cause of Buddhism, a very different religion which was introduced into Japan from India via Korea at the end of the sixth century, and is discussed under its own heading below. Shotoku Taishi commissioned the first Buddhist temple in Japan, the Asukadera, erected in 588 and paid for with the resources of the crown.

The word "Japan," the flag, and the national anthem

The Japanese had originally called their country "Yamato," but from the time of the late Kofun Period in the early seventh century, in an effort to promote the primacy of Japan at the expense of that of China, the Japanese began to call their nation Nihon, or Nippon. They elected to write that designation using two Chinese characters individually meaning "sun" and "source." The political intent was clear, because Japan's geographic location in the east of the Asian rim supported its claim as the "source of the rising sun." When these two Chinese characters are pronounced in Chinese, they are vocalized not as "nihon" but rather as "riben." The Chinese pronunciation was transliterated by Marco Polo in the thirteenth century as "Cipangu," which eventually became "Japan" in English and German, and "Japon" in French and Spanish.

This change of name reinforced the primacy of the sun in Japanese culture, and further emphasized the importance of Amaterasu, the sun goddess of Shinto, whose primacy in that pantheon was firmly established and who was believed to be the ancestor of all of Japan's emperors. Banners depicting the sun as their emblem were used by some of the noted families in Japan over 600 years ago, and when the ban against building large vessels was lifted following of Perry's visit in 1853–4, the Japanese recognized the need for a flag by which Japanese vessels might be recognized in international waters. The design for the present Japanese flag was suggested by Lord Shimazu Nariakira, the powerful head of the Satsuma clan in southern Japan. It depicts a large red circle on a white background, and is called the *Hinomaru* or "sun-circle." By official proclamation issued in 1870, the size and form of the flag, including the diameter of the sun and its placement within the white field, were strictly defined. The earliest public display of this flag as the national symbol of Japan occurred in 1860 on the occasion of the very first diplomatic delegation ever sent abroad by the Japanese government. That delegation arrived in the United States and the U.S. Navy cruiser *Powhattan* was placed at the disposal of the Japanese shogunate. The vessel flew the American flag from its stern and this Japanese flag from its bow. Some twelve years later in 1872, the *Hinomaru* was unfurled in a national ceremony for the very first time in Japan on the occasion of the opening of Japan's first railway by the Meiji emperor.

The nation's national anthem, *Kimigayo*, meaning, "The Reign of Our Emperor," consists of words taken from an ancient poem. Because this poem is so short, it was deemed necessary to repeat it two times.

> Thousands of years of happy reign be thine;
> Rule on, my lord, 'til what are pebbles now
> By age united to mighty rocks shall grow
> Whose venerable sides the moss doth line.

In 1860, John William Fenton, the Englishman who was the first bandmaster of the Japanese Army, composed a melody for *Kimigayo*, which he had adapted from an old Japanese theme. Then in 1881 a committee was appointed to select a more suitable melody, and that submitted by Hayashi Hiromori, a court musician, was substituted for that of Fenton. The revised melody was composed for traditional Japanese musical instruments, but it was soon determined to harmonize this piece according to the Western musical scale. The task fell upon Franz Eckert, a German bandmaster and Fenton's successor, who harmonized the melody to the Gregorian scale which was the basis of medieval European church music. It is for this reason that *Kimigayo* resounds with a moving religious solemnity. This version was performed for the first time during the celebration of the Meiji emperor's birthday in 1880, and was ultimately adopted as Japan's National Anthem in 1888.

Buddhism

Buddhism developed in North India from the teachings of Gautama (about 563–483 B.C.), the historic Buddha. The fundamental principles of Gautama's doctrine regarded the world as a place of universal suffering brought about by twin, basic human impulses, namely desire and acquisitiveness. Enlightenment, or a release from this state of worldly suffering, could be achieved by adherence to an eightfold program, the points of which consisted of right views, right intentions, right speech, right action, right livelihood, right effort, right mindfulness, and right concentration. The path to enlightenment was somewhat complicated by the principle of *karma*, a cause and effect theorem, which wove all acts of previous existences inextricably into the fabric of universal suffering which predestined individuals to several additional cycles of life, death, and rebirth before a true enlightenment and the concomitant release from suffering could be achieved. Influential as the teachings of Gautama were, his principles were substantially modified about a half a millennium after his death by the development of Mahayana, the Buddhism of the "Greater Vehicle."

According to this adjusted doctrine, the earlier form of Buddhism, now termed Hinayana, or "the Lesser Vehicle," was derided because its basic thrust was an instructional program by which individuals might find release from this perpetual cycle of death and rebirth. Within this system, Mahayana maintains, enlightenment could only be attained by those few capable of correctly adhering to the eight-point program. Plumbing ancient scripture, the adherents of Mahayana declared that just prior to his death Gautama had revealed the ultimate truth, namely that all living beings might potentially achieve enlightenment or Buddhahood. With this change of focus from the select few to the universal, the Mahayana doctrine also modified the prevailing view of the character of Gautama himself. He was transformed from a moral being into a transcendent entity who had the potential of attaining enlightenment because he had satisfied all the requirements to do so, but demurred. His postponed entry into Buddhahood was altruistic so that he could assist beings in their attempts to be released from the cycle of life, death, and rebirth. His motivation for this selfless effort was ascribed to his deep compassion for all living things. The entity possessed of this deferred potential to attain enlightenment was a new figure called the bodhisattva, "the Buddha-to-be."

The mind of one just introduced to the Mahayana School of Buddhism boggles when confronted with the bewildering complexities of its pantheon of different Buddhas and exalted beings. These complexities are the result of the development of Buddhism itself, one inherent principle of which was the successive reincarnation of beings. To these were then added deities adopted from other religions and regions in which Buddhists lived and practiced. The nature and character of these deities, principally from Hinduism but also from other religions of the Near East, were then adapted to Buddhist principles. In an attempt to bring some semblance of order to this pantheon, the Mahayana School promulgated the doctrine of the three forms of Buddha. The first was his all-embracing cosmic form. The second was his transcendent form, but even this consisted of different hypostases such as the Healing Buddha (called Yakushi in Japan), the Buddha of the Future (Miroku), the Buddha of Boundless Light (Amida), and so forth. The third was his transformation form, defined as the body he assumed when the Buddha existed on earth as Gautama, who is known as Shaka in Japan. One must, therefore, always bear in mind the potential for infinite permutations which were in fact developed by disparate sects of Buddhism once the religion was established throughout the archipelago in the Kamakura Period (discussed below). It was during this period as well that Zen Buddhism was adopted and became identified as the religion of the samurai class (also discussed below).

In keeping with the three forms of Buddha, representations are likewise varied, and the gestures of the hands can be found in a number of different attitudes, termed *mudras*. One will, therefore, restrict the discussion of these representations to that of the historical Buddha. In general, these images show him with one up-raised hand encouraging worshippers to allay their fears while the open palm of the other hand is a sign of charity. Very often there is a marked protuberance on the forehead as well as a third eye. These are signs connoting extraordinary wisdom and vision, respectively, and are among the twenty-three physical characteristics which according to the Mahayana School of Buddhism reflect the superhuman qualities of Gautama. The expression on his face is sometimes characterized by the "archaic smile," a phrase taken from descriptions of early Greek sculpture of the sixth century B.C.

Confucianism

Confucianism is the largely secular philosophy of life said to have been taught by Kong Qiu or Kong Fuzi, known to us in the Latinized form of his name Confucius (about 551–478 B.C.). Kong Qiu's thinking has been passed down in a number of different texts which sometimes put forward conflicting theories, and "Confucianism" does not consist of a uniform body of doctrines. Put simply, however, Confucius claimed that he was primarily concerned with practical and moral questions and that his main wish was to restore society to its original, virtuous, state. He believed in government by example and thought that rulers should be chosen for their moral qualities; if they failed to rule virtuously they would lose the "mandate of heaven" and should be deposed.

In the early Edo Period (seventeenth century), another aspect of Confucian teaching was used to bolster the authority of the newly-established shogunate or military government. This was Confucius's emphasis on hierarchical relations within the family and the state, making sons subservient to fathers, younger brothers subservient to older brothers, wives subservient to husbands and, especially in a Japanese context, samurai subservient to their lords. In the years immediately following the Meiji Restoration, when the shogunate lost power, Confucianism was benignly neglected by the authorities and its tenets discredited. However, Confucianism has been imbedded into the fabric of Japanese ethical thinking and the explication and discussion of moral values in contemporary Japan continues to be expressed in the lexicon of Confucianism.

NARA PERIOD (710–94)

Architecture is symbolic, and no more graphic manifestation of the transfer of the capital of the archipelago from the Asuka Valley to Nara can be adduced than the physical dismantling of the royal buildings at Fujiwara, the transport of their materials to Nara, and their subsequent reuse in the erection of new structures at the new capital. The reused building materials were still functional inasmuch as the older capital, Fujiwara, was only sixteen years old at the time its buildings were being dismantled for the use of their materials at Nara. The new capital, today called Nara but known as Heijokyo when it was established in the eighth century, was situated at the center of a newly created system of governmental roads which expedited travel by horse of imperial couriers and facilitated the transfer of taxable goods to the capital. The new city was itself designed on a grid pattern of streets intersecting one another at right angles, a type of city plan adopted from the Chinese and very similar to that developed independently by the ancient Greek architect Hippodamus of Miletus. The imperial palace was erected on land forming the northern limits of the city, which was itself the site of numerous Buddhist temples.

In fact, the Buddhist church was to play a significant role in the politics of the Nara Period because of the bifurcated nature of the government's administration. One branch comprised the imperial court, ruling from Nara and having centralized jurisdiction over a series of provincial centers in a system modeled on that of China's Tang Dynasty. The second branch was administered by the Todaiji, a temple granted the right by imperial decree of overseeing monasteries and nunneries in each provincial center. According to this dual system, temples were allowed to finance themselves because the state could not allocate funds from its own resources. The Todaiji Temple is not only the world's largest wooden building, but it is also the shrine enclosing the Daibutsu, or Great Buddha, representing the cosmic Buddha Vairocana, an image which is the world's largest bronze statue. It measures 53 feet in height and was completed in 749, having taken almost six years of labor to create following the order to do so by Emperor Shomu as "atonement" for a great epidemic of smallpox which ravaged the archipelago between 735–7. The technical challenges involved in the casting of this image laid the foundations for the tradition of bronze casting which was always thereafter in Japan intimately associated with the creation of Buddhist images and religious implements. These traditions were maintained and enabled Japanese metalsmiths to astonish Europe and America with their skills some 1,100 years later, as the examples of metalwork from the Meiji Era in this exhibition so admirably demonstrate. The eye-opening ceremony on the Daibutsu was performed in 752 when an Indian cleric was entrusted with painting the pupils of the effigy's eyes in order to imbue the image with symbolic life.

Although Emperor Shomu is rightly remembered as among the most devout of Buddhist emperors of Japan, the cultural brilliance of the Nara Period was not limited to such masterpieces of art and architecture. In fact, the period is characterized as well by a growing Japanese interest in other luxury crafts, many of which were imported during the Nara Period, not only from China but also from almost every nation in the known world. Fabrics of every description, household wares, glass, ceramics, two-dimensional works, and sculpture are but some of the imports which made their way to Japan from places as far afield as Arabia and Europe. The fabled Silk Routes were now effectively operational, and many of these objects were either copied or adapted in Japan by court-sponsored craftsmen whose activities, as well as the raw materials required for their finished products, were strictly regulated to ensure both stability and exclusivity of supply.

Soon after the establishment of Nara, imperial decree mandated the compilation of written histories. These constitute the earliest books ever written in Japan. They begin, as do the histories of other countries, with creation myths and legends, and gradually lose the veil of fiction to reveal the fabric of historical events the more recent in time the narrative reaches. This burst of literary activity was not limited to history, but included several compendia of poetry as well as geographical treatises concerned with several different provinces. Japanese literature was born.

HEIAN PERIOD (794–1185)

In 794 the Japanese Emperor Kanmu moved the capital from Nara to Heian-kyo, meaning "capital of peace and tranquility," later known as Kyoto, which more prosaically means simply the "capital city." Kyoto was to remain the capital of the archipelago until 1868 when it was replaced by Edo (renamed Tokyo) during the Meiji Restoration. Emperor Kanmu's motives for the transfer of the capital were numerous, but their unifying purpose was to fracture the infrastructure of his political and religious opponents. During the preceding Nara Period, the Fujiwara family had become dominant not only because it had established as hereditary the right to accede to the most important positions in the government, but also because it had consolidated that hereditary power base by arranging for the marriage of its women to princes and emperors, thus binding others to the larger Fujiwara clan, whose members were constantly engaged in internecine plots. The bifurcated nature of the country's administration during the Nara Period had provided the environment in which Buddhism flourished and in time Buddhist monks, because of their advantaged economic position, became political forces with which to contend, at times being complicit with this or that faction of the Fujiwara clan, while at others exercising independence aimed at depriving patrons and rivals alike of both prestige and power.

Kanmu took advantage of this complex situation. Indeed, he himself was elevated to the rank of emperor by members of a disaffected faction of the Fujiwara family who had arranged for the elimination under mysterious circumstances of a rival prince and his politically ambitious mother. Once enthroned, Kanmu sought to redress the abuses of the Buddhist monks and did so by refusing to allow their numbers to leave Nara and join him in Heian-kyo. Leaving these monks to their own devices in Nara enabled Kanmu to enlist the undivided attention of the secular nobility in the creation of the new capital. Factionalism was set aside as individuals now sought to curry the favor of the new ruler by expending their resources and energies on the new capital, which was likewise planned on a grid system but was greater in scale than Nara had been, measuring over two, and a half miles east to west and over three miles north to south.

The new political elite not only created a new city in Heian-kyo, but also restructured the government by reshaping Chinese legal precedents to conform to the political realities of Japan. In this political system, the emperor stood at the top of a pyramid-shaped administration representing a bureaucracy in which members were enrolled into eight basic offices, which were further divided into some thirty minutely defined posts. The rankings generally intermingled office with blood line so that the highest officials in the land were regarded as the most aristocratic, and these commanded the greatest wealth and resources. That wealth often took the form of lifetime grants by the emperor in the form of income from fixed parcels of rice fields, human chattels as either guards or servants, and even luxury goods such as silk.

Traditional histories of Japan have presented the Heian Period as a Golden Age, akin to Athens of the fifth century B.C. or Florence in the fifteenth century. Although such comparisons have become unfashionable, there is no doubt that the tenth and eleventh centuries witnessed Japan's greatest flowering of court culture, as manifest in the romantic literature of the period. The best example is doubtless *Genji monogatari* [The Tale of Genji], a very long novel written by Murasaki Shikibu, a lady-in-waiting at the court. Genji Hikaru, "the shining one," is the principal character, the son of an emperor born to a low-ranking concubine, who was to grow up and embody all the virtues prized by the sophisticated Heian Court. Genji was handsome and a great lover, a poet and calligrapher, a musician and dancer, and a gentleman possessed of great taste in a society which valued taste. The trysts of his youth are preceded by an elaborate etiquette of exchanged poems, written on perfumed stationery or fans often adorned with sprigs of flowers. *Makura no soshi* [The Pillow Book] also written by a lady-in-waiting, Sei Shonagon, is a collection of anecdotes, aphorisms, and personal opinions. The two works serve as an introduction to the extraordinary literary productivity of the Heian Period, which included lyric poetry as well. Buddhist architecture and sculpture also flourished. There are, unfortunately, few surviving masterpieces of lacquer, metalwork, or other applied arts, but the examples which are extant demonstrate that the Japanese craftspeople had broken out of their continental artistic shackles, imposed by models supplied by Korea and China, and had begun to create works of art with a distinctive identity.

Throughout the development of this political system, no one was capable of thwarting the political ambitions of the Fujiwara clan. One branch effectively gained control of the country by relying on the time-tested practice of intermarriage, particularly with members of the imperial family. Although polygamy was common, and many ambitious nobles aligned themselves through a series of marriages to sundry wives of the rich and powerful, the practice of uxorilocal marriage was advantageously exploited by the Fujiwara clan in arranging marriages for their women. According to this system the husband was obliged either to visit or to reside in his wife's house. That arrangement placed both husband, as well as all potential children from the union, under the direct control of the wife's father or brothers. In time the system would empower women economically because such marriages could increase their status and wealth. Nevertheless, this temporary economic empowerment could not erode the universally maintained principle of male primogeniture, the tenets of which excluded women initially from certain rights of inheritance (although that would change with time). More importantly, universal adherence to that principle prevented all women from becoming the *de jure* heads of their respective families, which meant in practice that no woman would become a sole monarch, ruling in her own right.

As this branch of the Fujiwara grew in prestige, wealth, and power, its members created a remarkable new office, that of *shikken* [regent] occupied by the male head of the branch, through which he exercised direct control over the emperor and his policies. Throughout the later Heian Period, the office of regent was used to further the cause of the Fujiwara, often to the point of elevating one of its younger sons to the position of emperor. Such a political system could not sustain itself without the absolute exploitation of both the agrarian population and its land. That exploitation was achieved with the gradual introduction of such agronomic practices as double-cropping by which wheat and rice were alternated as crops, and with technological developments such as the use of iron as the material for the manufacture of hoes and other implements, and the introduction of water-driven mortars. Productivity increased as these advances were systematically applied to reclaim tracts of land not previously under cultivation. Individuals were given title in perpetuity to lands newly brought under cultivation and certain others were granted tax immunity both for other tracts of land and for those who worked them. These factors contributed to the creation of the *shoen*, defined as aggregate tracts held by absentee landowners who sought to benefit from the tax exempt status enjoyed by such reclaimed lands. In time, the interests of the *shoen* came into conflict with those of owners of taxable lands, and a complex system developed, to the detriment of the state, whereby taxable land might deviously be incorporated into existing *shoen* or other tax exempt properties, such as that held by religious establishments, to avoid responsibility for fiscal levies.

All the while the military estate was extending imperial control throughout the vast reaches of the archipelago. An emperor might well rule in "the capital of peace and tranquility" as long as the military supported the central government and the bureaucrats remained content with their respective lots in life. Such a symbiotic existence, however, did not last for long. The general prosperity of the period enabled disaffected members of the imperial family, including those who had been forced to abdicate, to establish their own provincial pockets of power. Their rise was concomitant with the rise of provincial military families. Neither of these two recently emergent estates accepted the legitimacy of the emperor in the capital, and soon the provincial aristocracy recognized the necessity of an alliance with the provincial military as a means of asserting themselves at the expense of the central authority. The regional militias which Emperor Kanmu had sought to disband in the years immediately before his accession to the throne were once again in the ascendant. Armed rebellions were soon born, and private armies joined in the conflicts. And so it was that by the end of the period, the once mighty Fujiwara family had become dependent upon provincial warriors for enforcing their policies. It had initially hoped to be able to prevail by pitting one set of rivals against another. This policy met with incipient success but the court could not divide and conquer the families of the Taira and the Minamoto, whose combined might eclipsed that of the court. The members of the Taira family now prevailed, and attempted to administer its newly won realm by occupying the principal bureaucratic offices and implementing policy through the preexisting court structures. Go-Shirakawa, the emperor whom the Taira family had dislodged, then prevailed upon his former foe, the defeated Minamoto family, to redouble its efforts against the Taira. The overture was accepted and, after regrouping in eastern Japan under Yoritomo, a young general, the Minamoto renewed the conflict, known as the Genpei Wars, after the characters used to write parts of the proper names Taira and Minamoto. Their struggle lasted from 1156–85, after which time the Minamoto emerged victorious. The Genpei Wars were to enjoy posthumous commemoration as the source of a vast body of heroic myth and legend that formed a treasure-trove of subject matter for craftsmen during the Edo Period and Meiji Era.

Minamoto no Yoritomo, the successful warrior, assumed the title *Seii-tai-shogun*, literally meaning "barbarian-quelling generalissimo," which was subsequently abbreviated *shogun*, or "general." This title had been awarded to senior officials on various occasions since the eighth century, but from the end of the twelfth century it became the traditional title for the hereditary military dictators who were to control Japan for most of the next seven hundred years. Minamoto no Yoritomo established his military capital at Kamakura, not far from modern Yokohama, and is credited with forming the first *bakufu*, or "warrior government," a hierarchy initially based on his own supremacy and that of his immediate vassals, but the system was soon extended to define the legal status of every member of society, although emperors did continue to reign. The *bakufu*, while recognizing the right of an emperor to rule, was the *de facto* authority in Japan and only real power. Its manipulations of the person and office of the emperor may be regarded as an extension of similar policies established in this regard by the regents of the preceding Heian Period.

Towards the end of the thirteenth century, the leader of the *bakufu*, Hojo Tokimune, recognized the inability of the imperial court to organize the defense of the country against the impending invasions of the Mongols, the first of which reached Japan in 1274, and was defeated. As described above the Mongols returned in 1281, but a typhoon destroyed many of their vessels, and the force retreated from its established beach-head. Although the Mongols' planned third invasion never materialized because of the death of their leader Khubilai Khan in 1294, the *bakufu* steadfastly retained its control over the country for the next few years on the pretext of the necessity of maintaining the nation's military state of preparedness. The Hojo family had now supplanted the Minamoto as the dominant military power of the land.

On occasion, the court and the emperor openly warred against the *bakufu*, but with limited success. Nevertheless, the Kamakura Period came to an end with just such a war. In the 1320s resistance to the *bakufu* centered around Emperor Go-Daigo, who managed to rally a number of powerful warrior families, including the Ashikaga and the Hojo, to his cause. Their combined forces overthrew the *bakufu* in 1333, and established Go-Daigo as both the *de facto* and *de jure* ruler of Japan. His direct, but brief rule of Japan was to last but three years.

Zen Buddhism

Zen Buddhism was first developed in China by a quasi-historical figure named Bodhidharma, reputedly an Indian priest in the sixth century, but it was not firmly established in Japan until the Kamakura Period. *Zen*, literally "meditation," is a fundamental cornerstone of Buddhism in general, and often involves sitting in a kneeling position which is very difficult to sustain for long periods. Even Gautama, it is believed, achieved Buddhahood while in a deeply meditative state. In the Zen School of Buddhism, *satori*, "enlightenment," occurs when beings realize that the objectives of their worldly quest–wealth and power–and the subsequent cause of their suffering are not real. Wealth and power are illusions. Enlightenment can only be achieved, therefore, via meditation through a program combining effort and discipline. In much the same way that the philosophy of Buddhism allowed for differing interpretations which resulted in the development of the Greater and Lesser Vehicles, so, too, the nature of Zen was susceptible to varying interpretations which contributed to the doctrinal differences responsible for dividing Zen Buddhism into two major sects during the Kamakura Period. Proponents of the Rinzai School of Zen maintain that *satori* could be achieved suddenly, whereas their antagonists of the Soto School of Zen argue that enlightenment can only be attained gradually after a prolonged process of *zazen*, "seated meditation." If anyone–especially an Occidental–neither raised in a Zen environment nor conversant with the philosophy of Zen and its tenets seeks to learn about the nature of *satori* from a Zen master, the learning process may be impeded by purposeful obfuscation bordering on the ridiculous. It was not uncommon for a Zen master to reply to questions about the nature of *satori* by stating simply, "three pounds of flax." Such a reply was not intended to be interpreted in order to plumb its symbolic meaning, but was offered to demonstrate that Zen *satori* could never be explained because it could only be directly experienced, and even then only through meditation via a program of effort and discipline. It is perhaps of interest to note that Eisai (1141–1215), who introduced the Rinzai School of Zen Buddhism to Japan was responsible for the renewed consumption of tea which ultimately led to the codification of the etiquette regulating *chanoyu*, the tea ceremony.

A curious mythology has developed in the West with regard to Zen Buddhism as it relates to the samurai warrior class of Japan's medieval period. This rather romantic notion attempts to link the Zen school's advocacy of self-discipline and self-control with a putative samurai ethic emphasizing the same qualities. This same notion egregiously stresses simplicity and a directness of communication linking Zen Buddhism to a kind of anti-intellectualism. While it is true that the overwhelming proportion of samurai warriors during this period of Zen's acceptance were rude, illiterate individuals engaged in the savage business of warfare, it does not follow that their perceived anti-intellectualism was the dominant factor responsible for their embrace of Zen Buddhism. Closer examination of the religious inclinations of this period reveals that the average samurai warrior was more personally involved in new salvationist sects. What colors this samurai epoch with Zen hues is that fact that society's shakers and movers, the ruling members of samurai society, embraced Zen Buddhism. Zen priests in this medieval period of Japan's history took a keen interest in matters intellectual and cultural, traveling back and forth to the continent on a regular basis, and returning each time with cultural borrowings which were subsequently adapted by the Japanese. The impact of Zen Buddhism on Japanese culture–*suibokuga* [monochromatic ink-painting], *kare sansui* ["dry landscapes" or rock gardens], *No* theater, and *chanoyu* [tea ceremony]–is discussed later in this chapter.

MUROMACHI PERIOD (1333–1568)

The brief reign of Emperor Go-Daigo was brought to an end because his advocacy of the supremacy of the central government directly controlled by the person of the emperor could not be countenanced by the warrior class which had brought him to power. In 1336 Ashikaga Takauji forced Go-Daigo to flee to the Yoshino region south of Kyoto, assumed the title of *shogun*, and formed a second warrior government, known as the Muromachi *bakufu*, installing a puppet emperor in the process. For the next thirty years, Japan was engaged in a civil war between the faction supporting the ousted Emperor Go-Daigo and his successors and that supporting his foe, the shogun Ashikaga Takauji. That neither side was able to prevail for so long a period of time was a harbinger of things to come because for the next two centuries Japan was to become fragmented into a series of small military enclaves. The genesis of this military fragmentation of the land can be principally attributed to the initial need of the members of the Ashikaga shogunate to ally itself with local vassals and provincial military governors, because they lacked extensive holdings of land and adequate military power of their own. Actual power, however, was eventually concentrated in the hands of a large number of regional feudal lords, the *daimyo* [literally "great name"]. By the end of this period, there were no less than 250 domains, each headed by a feudal warlord, scattered throughout the land. Incessant civil wars, now commonplace, were to continue into the sixteenth century. As these estates selfishly interacted with one another for their own advancement, a principle of power was developed into the ethical system to which the members of the warrior class subscribed. Heroism, loyalty, and a willingness to die for one's lord became the mottos of the day, proclaimed by the *daimyo*, and enshrined in moving tales of war such as those recounted in the *Heike monogatari* [*The Tales of the Heike*], another name by which the Taira clan was known. Vassals were bound to lords by this honor system, backed by force of arms which controlled relatively small domains, dominated by defensible castles, and maintained by a warrior class ready and able to defend or to attack in an instant.

Daimyo castles became focal points around which towns developed, as they also did around temples. These population pockets were then connected by the development of a network of long-distance communications by both land and sea, and trade began to flourish, not only overland but also overseas.

This maritime commerce fostered the development of towns along the coasts of the archipelago. Despite the lack of a central government, Japan experienced rapid economic growth. Money now replaced barter as the accepted medium of exchange. Craft workers gained improved status, furthering their interests through the establishment of *za*, organizations similar to the medieval European craft guilds. Most of their production was directed to the warrior class, and those products included the tools of war, foremost among which was the manufacture of swords, but also of helmets and other types of body armor as well as horse trappings. These implements combined the highest levels of technical achievement with consummate aesthetic considerations.

Society was now being so transformed that some of the more enduring social and cultural characteristics of the land which have become most closely associated with the West's image of Japan began to take root and grow. So, for example, in 1191 the priest Eisai returned from a visit to China and introduced the country not only to the meditative form of Buddhism called Zen but also to the practice of drinking an infusion from the leaves of the tea plant and to *chanoyu*, the tea ceremony, a kind of formalized social gathering that is still widely popular today. Zen monasteries developed rapidly in both Kyoto and Kamakura, and Zen philosophy combined with martial codes developed during the twelfth-century wars to form the samurai ethical system later codified as *bushido*, literally, "the way of the warrior."

At the same time the *daimyo* and their retainers developed the other arts so necessary for social intercourse and the administration of their domains. Some were accomplished poets in their own right, others excelled in various fields of the fine arts, and all were lavish patrons of culture. Palaces and other aristocratic residences began to be decorated with screens and wall paintings. Buddhist monks were becoming a fixed feature of this emergent civilizing movement. Literary salons were a common feature of the times in which monk, *daimyo*, and warrior communed with one another on equal terms. Much of the impetus for this cultural flowering of the arts was a direct result of the introduction of Zen which not only provided the shogunate with a much needed ideology, but together with some other less austere devotional sects of Buddhism inspired a renaissance in the visual and performing arts, including ink-painting, rock gardens, *No* theater, and the tea ceremony.

Ink painting

The form of monochromatic painting known as *suibokuga* was indebted to traditions developed over several centuries by Chinese artists, especially those of the Song (960–1279) and Yuan (1280–1368) Dynasties; its brushwork was derived from techniques developed first by calligraphers. Although Japanese artists initially devoted themselves to portrait and figural studies, in time their primary subject matter was *sansui*, landscapes dominated by mountains and flowing water. Some commentators have maintained that *suibokuga* gained favor in medieval Japan because its dependence on monochromatic black ink struck the familiar chords of the period's predilection for the cold and the lonely.

Kare-sansui

The medieval period also witnessed the introduction of *kare-sansui,* literally "withered landscapes," in the form of dry rock gardens which are habitually erected in the grounds of Zen temples. In some instances the designs of these gardens reflect an inherent Japanese love of miniaturization, as also seen in bonsai. Large rocks may come to represent massive mountain ranges, or islands set into seas frozen in time, their waves and currents neatly created by the tines of a rake. Connoisseurs see a marked similarity between the aesthetics of *kare-sansui* and *suibokuga*, the abstract quality of both reflecting a constant in the medieval Japanese aesthetic and soul which gravitates toward the cold and the lonely. It is not surprising to learn, therefore, that some of the medieval period's leading exponents of *suibokuga* were equally famous for their designs of dry rock gardens.

No theater

The *No* [literally, "talent" or "ability"] theater probably had its origins in the distant past but was indebted to an amalgam of influences both foreign and domestic, aristocratic and plebeian. During the early medieval period, theatrical entertainment's two most popular forms were *sarugaku* and *dengaku. Sarugaku*, literally "monkey music," is an art form which has defied all attempts at definition, although an educated guess proposes that the actors may have performed comic-like acrobatics and the like. *Dengaku*, literally "field music," is easier to define because it is ultimately based on the types of singing and dancing performed by villagers in the fields during the harvest. In time the fine line distinguishing the one form of performance from the other virtually vanished, but in contemporary records mentions of *dengaku* seem to predominate.

The development of the *No* theater can be directly ascribed to the shogun Ashikaga Yoshimitsu (1358–1408), who attended a *dengaku* performance in 1374, the principals of which were Kan'ami (1333–84) and his son, Zeami (1363–1443). So enamored of the art form was Yoshimitsu that he became excessive in his financial patronage of the father and son. The two were suddenly elevated into the rarified cultural ambiance of the court at Kyoto. In such an environment and with such backing, Kan'ami and Zeami soon transformed *dengaku* into what has come to be known as classic *No* theater. They were not only actors, but also playwrights, and many of the enduring masterpieces of *No* theater created at that time can be confidently ascribed to the genius of the one or the other. Zeami, the son, was also a critic of discriminating taste and his surviving commentaries provide an extraordinary window on to the landscape of medieval Japan's aesthetic tastes to which he himself had contributed.

One modern critic has defined *No* as "a dramatic poem concerned with remote or supernatural events, performed by a dancer, often masked, who shares with lesser personages and a chorus the singing and declamation of the poetry." To many an Occidental audience, a *No* performance comes across as tedious, taking what appears to be an eternity to resolve a seemingly nonexistent plot. Reality does not matter in *No* where the performers are universally male. What is of concern is the ability of the actor to convey in a convincing manner the mystery and depth of the most treasured aesthetic of the medieval age. *No* plays are divided into five categories: about gods, about warriors, about women, about miscellaneous affairs, and about demons; and enjoy renewed popularity today as an art form.

Chanoyu [the tea ceremony]

Tea as a beverage had been introduced into Japan from China as early as the ninth century. The Buddhist priest Eisai (above), who is better known as the founder of the Rinzai School of Zen Buddhism, is said to have reintroduced the Japanese to tea on a grand scale in the medieval period when he recommended it for medicinal purposes, and recognized its antisoporific properties which kept acolytes awake during their prolonged meditative training periods. By the fourteenth century, the Japanese were drinking tea for its taste, rather than as a pharmaceutical, and soon developed a social custom–not too different from today's wine tasting affairs–in which contestants would sip tea not only to demonstrate their ability to identify the specific type or blend of tea brewed but also to judge both its quality and that of the water used. In time, special attention was paid as well to the objects used for the brewing of the tea and its serving. But the *chanoyu* was only developed as a standardized, formal ceremony during the time of the shogun Ashikaga Yoshimasa (1435–90), who entrusted three men of discriminating taste with the discharge of his cultural affairs. Among the three was Noami (1397–1471) who combined into one room the preparation and consumption of the tea, the proper handling of the utensils, and even the comportment of the servers which in many ways imitated the movement of actors in the *No* theater.

The ceremony was further refined by Murata Juko (1422–1502), a merchant from Nara and enthusiastic student of Zen Buddhism. It was not until the sixteenth century, however, that the highest form of the tea ceremony, *wabicha*, was developed. So that one is not seduced into thinking that the tea ceremony simply involves brewing and serving, it must be noted that the environment in which the ceremony is performed, often in the form of an independent tea house, is an integral part of the ceremony. In many ways, words fail to explain adequately the cultural depth of the tea ceremony. In the end, one is forced to revert to the gnomic utterances of Sen no Rikyu (1520–91), perhaps the greatest tea master of all, who once mysteriously said that *chanoyu* was simply a matter of "boiling water, making tea, and drinking it." In much that same way that *satori* is an individual achievement which is not susceptible to verbal explication, the tea ceremony must be experienced because it cannot be described.

The first Europeans in Japan

The period of incessant warfare, the so-called *sengoku jidai*, "the era of the country at war" (a phrase characteristically borrowed from early Chinese history), was brought to an end in the second half of the sixteenth century by the successive efforts of three warlords, but not before the arrival of the first Europeans in Japan began to exercise a considerable influence on Japanese culture. In 1543, three Portuguese sailors were shipwrecked on the island of Tanegashima off the coast of Kyushu. This was, after all, the European Age of Discovery. From that moment on, the warlords of Japan added European-style firearms to their arsenals, thereby greatly reducing the effectiveness of the samurai warrior's sword and tipping the balance of power in favor of those embracing the new technology. The governor of Tanegashima immediately recognized the superiority of these Portuguese weapons and, typical of the mimetic nature of certain aspects of Japanese culture, ordered his swordsmiths to replicate the arquebus. Within two decades, the firearms industry in Japan improved upon the spring and trigger mechanisms of their European prototypes, and also developed a covering for the firing mechanism which allowed one to shoot in the pouring rain or with impunity at night since the same covering design concealed the flare produced when the trigger was pulled. If the musket were to replace the sword, the Japanese samurai would have to adopt tactics germane to the firearm. Such adoption took three decades to become universal, and was the direct result of the Battle of Nagashino in 1575 when Oda Nobunaga's (1534–82) 3,000 musketeers annihilated the mounted, sword-wielding samurai warriors who charged their well-defended position. *Daimyo* were obliged not only to equip their warriors with firearms, but were compelled to improve the designs of their fortifications in order to withstand attacks from bullets and cannonballs.

Accompanying the firearm was the second of those European influences on Japan, in the form of the arrival of Christian missionaries, whose zealous numbers swelled after the arrival in 1549 of the Portuguese Jesuit, Francis Xavier. He was followed by a host of Jesuit missionaries intent on proselytizing the inhabitants, and their arrival was coincident with that of Portuguese traders. The Jesuits were followed in turn by both Franciscans and Dominicans. The arrival of these Christian missionaries in great numbers occurred precisely during this period of Japan's history when the power of the Ashikaga shoguns was at an all-time low, the person of emperor of little consequence, and obscure warriors were being catapulted to the summits of power, often usurping their lords' authority and status. The missionaries bore witness to these tumultuous times and recorded their observations in letters which were then read in Europe, thereby providing Christendom with its first, first-hand accounts of the life and customs of the people on these islands. The Jesuits, correctly recognizing the sheer numbers of *daimyo* competing for power, recorded what they saw, but incorrectly referred to these warlords as kings, giving contemporary Europeans the false impression that Japan was a confederation of princely kingdoms.

Although short-lived, the Momoyama Period witnessed the successive rule of three powerful war-lords, the first of whom was named Oda Nobunaga (above). He was in turn defeated by Toyotomi Hideyoshi (1536–98), under whose patronage the arts so flourished that the stage was set for the development of sophisticated urban craft workshops which were to remain active well into the Meiji Era. This remarkable flowering of the arts developed against the period's background of constant military strife. In 1600 the third of these warlords, Tokugawa Ieyasu (1542–1616), successfully defeated his rivals at the huge Battle of Sekigahara. Three years later, he established the eponymous Tokugawa shogunate as well as his capital at a little fishing village called Edo, in the same part of Japan as the earlier shogunal capital of Kamakura. This city's change of name from Edo to Tokyo, the "eastern capital," would be one of the most symbolic reforms of the early Meiji Era. With his siege of Osaka Castle in 1615 Ieyasu completed his conquest of Japan, and the archipelago was united under his banner.

In the early years of the Momoyama Period when wars between factions escalated, Ashikaga Yoshiteru, one of the last shoguns of the Muromachi Period, granted Gaspar Vilela the right to preach in Kyoto, Nara, and Sakai. A minor provincial warlord, Oda Nobunaga by name, who was to become effective ruler of Japan in 1573, was initially allied to Ashikaga Yoshiteru, and furthered the latter's incubation of Christianity in Japan. Nobunaga in turn was predisposed to patronizing the arts, and permitted Luis Frois, who had earlier penned his influential *History of Japan*, to erect a church in his capital, which was called Nanbanji, "the Temple of the Southern Barbarians." Nobunaga's motives for fostering Christianity were political because he viewed the Jesuits as a tool to combat the influence of Buddhists in his realm. The Jesuits, misreading his intentions, regarded Nobunaga's affability as a sign that he was their great protector. Nobunaga even went so far as to sponsor officially sanctioned debates between the Buddhists and the Jesuits.

The early Momoyama Period was a time of widespread Japanese contact with the Portuguese and the Dutch, and this included a rather unusual Japanese mission dispatched to Europe from 1582–1590. The mission was the brainchild of the Italian Jesuit Alessandro Valignano, chief of the Jesuit order in the Far East, and consisted of four young boys between the ages of twelve and thirteen from *daimyo* families who were enrolled as students in one of Japan's Jesuit seminaries. They were received both by King Philip II in Spain and by Pope Gregory XIII, they traveled to Venice, and were painted by Tintoretto. Thereafter they returned to Japan where their experiences had neither an immediate nor lasting effect. Nevertheless this mission demonstrates the extent to which Japan had quickly become an active player on the international scene.

But this era of good feeling toward the recently arrived Europeans soon changed, as an increasingly hostile attitude towards foreigners in general and Christianity in particular developed. The period's second ruler, Toyotomi Hideyoshi, began issuing edicts as early as 1587, the objectives of which were to restrict the practice of Christianity and expel the missionaries. The measures were not rigorously enforced, and even Hideyoshi received the four boys who had gone to Europe upon their return. However, these repressive measures were indications of harder times to come for practicing Christians in Japan. Hideyoshi's animus was not limited to religious opposition, but was also directed against other Asian nations. Having succeeded in his attempt to unify Japan, he aspired to establish an Asian empire centered in China. To that end, he invaded Korea in 1592, but the peninsula's resistance to Hideyoshi armies was heroic, and the dream of empire died with his death.

Official Japanese opposition to Christianity during this period must be regarded against the broader picture of international events in general and sectarian strife in the archipelago in particular. One turns first to the issue of that sectarian strife. Antagonism towards certain Japanese religious institutions which had grown over-powerful, such as Ishiyama Honganji (a temple of the Buddhist "True Pure Land" sect), was becoming commonplace. Within its vast temple precinct had grown an economically viable fortress-town, and the sect, possessed of its own secular aspirations, labeled Nobunaga "the great enemy of Buddhist law." It is within this broader picture of secular strife that one must regard Nobunaga's bloody removal of religious opposition to his rule. In 1571, for example, he was responsible for the massacre of the soldier-monks of the Tendai Sect and his protracted assault in 1580 humbled the Ishiyama Honganji.

Developments within Catholic Europe were also a factor in the rise of anti-Christian sentiment in Japan during this time. Contacts with Europe had informed the Japanese, however reliably may be debated, about the intense rivalry between the Jesuits and the Franciscans, perhaps resonating with the awareness of the existing competition among Japanese sects. Some Japanese may have even feared being dragged into this conflict to their detriment, while others were aware of the colonial policies of both Spain and Portugal in the New World. Japanese opposition to European Christianity may be regarded from several vantages, but one undeniably significant contribution to Japanese society by the Jesuits was their establishment of a printing press employing movable type. It was the same Valignano responsible for the Japanese boys' European trip who acknowledged this need and secured the importation into Japan from Europe of the first such equipment. Although his operation, the Jesuit Mission Press, was short-lived, its impact was extraordinary because it produced the first press runs created with metal, rather than wooden type, the first pages printed in Japanese cursive script, and the first illustrations made by copper engravings. The first ever example of printed secular Japanese literature was published by this firm as well. However, in part because of the cursive, continuous appearance of the Japanese syllabary called *hiragana* (above), movable types were soon abandoned in favor of carved woodblocks each used to print a whole page. The permanent change to movable metal types did not take place until the Meiji Era.

THE EDO OR TOKUGAWA PERIOD (1615–1868)

Tokugawa Ieyasu was the eponymous founder of a dynasty which was to rule Japan for the better part of the next three centuries. The Japan of the Momoyama Period had, by the end of the sixteenth century, degenerated into belligerent confrontations among *daimyo*, joined from time to time by peasant confederations and religious institutions. With no assertive central government, the factional divisions of the archipelago solidified into autonomous fiefdoms with passage between them severely restricted and lines of communication often truncated. Ambitious warlords, Tokugawa Ieyasu among them, played the political hand dealt for high stakes, as each aspired to become dominant. Military conquest became married to diplomacy, and both tools were used to erect alliances. Diplomacy and/or force soon enabled Ieyasu to assert his authority over larger areas of the archipelago, and with that increased authority came economic prosperity and fiscal consolidation. Recalcitrant religious institutions were incorporated into his ever-growing realm as their armies were defeated and their lands confiscated. Peace was brought to the countryside as successive peasant insurrections were quelled. Ieyasu had now become dominant, but his dominance was challenged by a coalition of his most powerful opponents, whose combined superior forces were defeated by Ieyasu's 70,000 in 1600 at the Battle of Sekigahara. Ieyasu took for himself the title *sei-i-taishogun*, literally, "commander-in-chief of the pacification of the savages," and proved to be an able administrator, setting into motion reforms which centralized the authority of the Tokugawa family as it successively assumed most of the functions ordinarily reserved for a national government. In addition to controlling the nation's currency and weights and measures, Ieyasu also took control of large sections of real estate in the archipelago which even included the cities of Edo (later to be known as Tokyo), his capital, Kyoto, the emperor's residence, Osaka, the nation's commercial center, and Nagasaki, the nation's seat of international commerce and diplomacy. The administration which he had thus established came to be known as the *bakufu*, the same designation as had earlier been applied to that of the Kamakura and Muromachi Periods (above).

Ieyasu also put in place a complex set of arrangements designed to keep the *daimyo* in their place and stabilize his new administrative order. The Japanese feudal nobility was divided into three categories–*shinpan*, *fudai*, and *tozama*–according to their relationship to Ieyasu's family. The *shinpan* were the closest and consisted of three cadet branches of the Tokugawa clan. Next came the *fudai*, trusted families who had thrown in their lot with the all-conquering Ieyasu before the climactic Battle of Sekigahara, and last the *tozama*, enemies of the Tokugawa who had been subjugated either during or after Sekigahara, including some of Japan's richest feudal potentates. Under a system called *sankin kotai*, "attendance by turn," the *daimyo* were obliged to spend one year in every two at Edo. They were further obliged to leave their womenfolk there as hostages, and were consequently compelled into devoting a large part of their wealth to maintaining luxurious establishments in the capital and making expensive ceremonial journeys to and from their domains, often many hundreds of miles away. Not only did this system consolidate Tokugawa control, it also provided a dependable living for a range of craftspeople, including lacquerers, weavers and, above all, metalworkers who created and embellished the swords which were the proudest possessions of the *daimyo* and their samurai vassals. The position of the *daimyo* was thus maintained, and they continued to rely upon the services of samurai warriors. It is to the samurai of this period that we now turn.

The samurai

One of the salient characteristics of this administration was its excessive reliance upon samurai warriors, who at the beginning of the period provided the military might and power needed to secure the position of the Tokugawa family, as exercised not only by their members but also by the *daimyo* who served under them. Although Buddhism and Shinto continued to play a key role in national life, Confucianism formed the ideology of the Tokugawa shogunate. Confucianism was useful to the shoguns because of the emphasis it placed on decorum and the maintenance of correct hierarchical and family relationships. It also provided the basis for the division of Japanese society into the four ranks of *shi-no-ko-sho*, samurai (of all kinds from shogun to petty retainer), peasants, workmen and merchants. In time these samurai became more beneficial to the administration as bureaucrats rather than as warriors, particularly since the archipelago under the Tokugawa regime was eventually to enjoy almost two centuries of relative peace. Despite this change of function, the martial character of the period fostered a rather romantic notion of the samurai which stood in ironic juxtaposition to the real role which they were now fulfilling. The period developed a specific ideology, *bushido*, literally "the way of the warrior," which extolled the high-minded ethics of an idealized class of non-warring warriors whose members were now for the most part desk-bound civil servants, dependent upon the state for their income. Nevertheless, *bushido* placed an excessive reliance on the blind devotion of a samurai to his lord even to the point of death, if it furthered the lord's cause. Such devotion demanded Spartan discipline, self-sacrifice, and a wholesome character. These ideal samurai were to avoid the *carpe diem* lifestyle of eating, drinking, and being merry.

Within such a glorified ethos, the institution of a samurai-staffed bureaucracy simultaneously created liabilities which were to so plague the administration of the Edo Period that they were only redressed by the reforms of the Meiji Restoration of 1868. Some of these abuses were endemic to the system because the Tokugawa administration, although it did succeed in uniting Japan, was unable to dismantle the entrenched client-patron system. The samurai-based administration at the top relied upon numerous smaller samurai-based administrations in the hands of the *daimyo*. Whereas all reaped the benefits of the Tokugawa domestic peace, the local *daimyo* were assiduous in promoting their local areas and did not subordinate their personal interests to the benefit of the archipelago as a whole. This local, self-interested aggrandizement fostered the growth of hereditary offices which not only replaced all semblance of a merit system but also developed checks prohibiting those not born into various administrative systems from ever joining those ranks. Soon, only those born into samurai families could become samurai, and this system of following in one's father's footsteps was gradually extended in theory to encompass all members of society as a whole regardless of avocation. Furthermore, the Tokugawa *bakufu* faced a series of economic recessions that were precipitated in part by its inability to tax the archipelago effectively. Local *daimyo* syphoned off revenues for their own purposes, while both the *bakufu* and the *daimyo* were forced to underwrite the escalating costs of maintaining a samurai-based bureaucracy whose ranks swelled with each passing year. This bleak economic picture was exacerbated by the widely-held belief that the country's fiscal interests ought to be rooted in subsistence agriculture.

The urbanization of Japan

During the Edo Period, Japan was among the most highly urbanized nations of the pre-modern world: Edo, the capital, became the most populous city on earth, with over one million inhabitants. Despite this degree of urbanization, the traditional bias toward subsistence agriculture and its peasant farmers promoted a governmental prejudice against the *chonin*, the merchant class of the big cities, resulting in repeated efforts to curtail their economic activities and limit the size of the sprawling urban centers. Despite repressive measures commerce did flourish, as did resentment because the merchants, regarded as being the lowest social status in the theoretical hierarchy promoted by the shogunate, were for the most part actually better off than their social superiors, the samurai.

This economic growth, tied to urbanization, altered the fabric of the subsistence agriculture which many Japanese had come to revere. On the one hand, the established local administrations and extended period of relative peace left the peasant farmers in relative isolation, free to follow their own inclinations, foremost of which was tax evasion, another factor contributing to the economic decline of the Tokugawa *bakufu*. On the other hand, the urban masses demanded foodstuffs, and that need was supplied by farmers who now supplanted rice as the crop of choice with others eagerly consumed by the *chonin*. The picture of the subsistence peasant, dutifully growing rice with which to pay his taxes and raising just enough in the way of other crops to sustain his kinfolks, now gave way to these new market forces. Agriculture had now become a commercial enterprise, but one with serious consequences for Japanese society. The first was in the form of take-overs, as ambitious individuals gobbled up the arable land of their less fortunate compatriots, and the second was the resulting divorcing from the land of now landless laborers. In the long term, all of these contradictions between the theoretical scheme and the realities of economic life proved to be a major source of political instability.

The "Floating World"

A curious phenomenon of the culture of the Edo Period was the reinterpretation of the medieval Buddhist definition of the word *ukiyo*, literally "floating world." Because Buddhism maintained that beings were constantly engaged in a state of worldly suffering as they sought release in enlightenment, life was fundamentally sad. As they moved from one state to another, their existence in any one life might be characterized as both insubstantial and ever-changing. In the Edo Period *ukiyo* was redefined to conform to the social realities of the times. To begin with, the members of the samurai class, while still distinguished by sword, coiffure, and costume, were now for the most part desk-bound bureaucrats, not fierce warriors. Their milieu had been transformed from the countryside to the urban sprawl of Japan's ever-growing cities with their booming pre-capitalist economies. Money, rather than status, rank or birth was what mattered. Growing financial independence enabled urban Japan to develop a more modern concept of leisure. In Japan's traditional agricultural society work had ceased only for the celebration of religious festivals or the ceremonies surrounding birth, marriage, and death. Money as surplus conspired with the development of large urban areas to redefine one aspect of Buddhism's *ukiyo*. Whereas the concept of ever-changing existence still remained fundamental to its definition, pleasure replaced sadness as the key ingredient of the definition because the world was now charged with a varied and mutable menu of physical pleasures. Entertainment quarters, which can be compared to certain "red-light districts" in today's urban areas, began to take root. Each city had such an area, be it the Yoshiwara in Edo [Tokyo], the Shinmachi in Osaka, or the Shimabara of Kyoto. Each was appointed with myriad brothels, theaters, tea houses, public baths, palaces of leisure where one could indulge sensuous pleasures. This transformation of the Buddhist concept of *ukiyo* was incongruent with the tenets of Confucianism, but it was perhaps for this very reason that the pleasure quarters were so popular. Their services enabled one to escape, however temporarily, from the shackles of social decorum and rigorous, individual behavior which Confucian restraints imposed. Yet it must be said that although government officials exercised diligence in monitoring these districts, those engaged in the trades plied there did much to police their own activities. The floating worlds did much to dismantle the social hierarchy of Japan, because one's standing as a patron of any establishment was governed by the amount of one's expendable, discretionary income and sensitivity to aesthetic or cultural nuance, rather than on status or rank within society.

Kabuki

The word *kabuki,* denoting daring behavior bordering on the improper, was first applied by the Japanese to an art form developed by Okuni, a woman of obscure origins living around 1600, who may have been at one time a Shinto shrine attendant. She led a troupe of female dancers in a novel form of outdoor musical entertainment which soon became such a commercial success that it spawned competing groups of performers. Their repertoire included *nenbutsu* dancing, originally an ecstatic religious song and dance performed by devotees of the Amida Buddha, which had since become absorbed into the folk dances of Japan. In addition, her troupe performed a series of satirical skits which recreated trysts between men and prostitutes in a variety of settings, and did so with a such degree of verisimilitude, because many of the performers were themselves practicing prostitutes, that the government banned female *kabuki* altogether in 1629. That ban propelled young men's *kabuki* onto center-stage, but the comportment of these young men on stage were perceived to arouse such homoerotic passions in the audience that these too were banned in 1652. Henceforth, only adult males, or youths who could pass for adults, were allowed to perform in *kabuki*. Because of the prohibition against female actresses, female roles were assumed by *onnagata*, specialist male performers whose highly stylized performances continue, even today, to capture the essence of feminine movement both on and off stage. Until *kabuki* became a more respectable and officially-recognized art form, a development that did not occur until the Meiji Era, playwrights tended to assume a very subservient role, their complicated plots and scripts serving simply as a vehicle for theatrical display by the leading actors. Music, dance, spectacular action sequences, stage-tricks, and highly mannered poses called *mie* are major components of most traditional *kabuki* performances, which could often last for the best part of an entire day and include several different plays. The top *kabuki* actors commanded enormous public admiration, not only for their dramatic skill but also as arbiters of popular taste. They were very frequently depicted by woodblock print artists (below) and, as the Edo Period drew on, their extravagant public behavior often brought them into conflict with the shogunal authorities. Despite its popular origins, *kabuki* today has increasing difficulty in attracting younger audiences who are more interested in forms of entertainment that are the same as, or equivalent to, those enjoyed by their peers in America and Europe.

Bunraku

Almost as popular as *kabuki* in its day was the *bunraku* or *joruri* puppet drama (*bunraku*, the term used today, is derived from the name of a nineteenth-century theater manager), which made its first recognizable appearance in the seventeenth century. The three elements that go to make up *joruri* are the large (about four feet high) puppets, the text chanted by a single reciter, and the accompaniment on the *shamisen*, a three-stringed plucked musical instrument introduced from the Ryukyu Islands to Japan in the sixteenth century. The mature form of the drama achieved overwhelming popularity during the first half of the Edo Period, especially in Kyoto and Osaka, thanks to the talents of the dramatist Chikamatsu Monzaemon (1653–1725), sometimes called "the Shakespeare of Japan," and the chanter Takemoto Gidayu (1651–1714). In this form, each major puppet is manipulated on the thirty-six foot stage by three operators standing in a trench. The operators are not hidden but the audience easily ignores them, so lifelike are the puppets they operate by means of sticks and internal springs.

Ikebana

Leisure in Japan also took several directions that were more didactic and educational and were (and still are) considered to be morally useful occupations, described as *do* (pronounced "doe"), meaning "a way," including *chado* or *sado* [the way of tea], *shodo* [the way of calligraphy], and *kado*, [the way of flowers], better known as *ikebana*. There are many styles of *ikebana* and each is promoted by a separate school headed by an *iemoto* or grand master, a term also used for the heads of tea ceremony and other traditional cultural organizations. The arrangement of flowers follows strict rules for representing heaven, earth, and people. Some styles are extremely simple, others are very complex, bordering on the extravagant. Today, there are over 3,000 *ikebana* schools in Japan with a combined enrollment of more than 15 million students.

Origami

In this connection it may be worthwhile mentioning *origami* [literally "folded paper"], a very popular pastime in which squares of colored paper are folded into different shapes. Dogs, birds, gorillas, and an array of inanimate objects can be made from a single piece of paper. *Origami* cranes are often offered in huge numbers at Shinto shrines, and a popular tradition dictates that when a person is very sick, friends and relatives often fold a thousand *origami* cranes as a prayer for the person's recovery or repose. Today, this pastime is so popular that *origami* associations have sprung up in seventeen different countries.

THE QUESTION OF ISOLATION

In order to understand the events which led to the Meiji Restoration of 1868, it is necessary to consider the issue of isolation as it relates to Japan in the Tokugawa or Edo Period. We have already seen how Japanese intercourse with the West began as a result of the eastward spread of the European "Age of Discoveries" which reached Japan in 1543, when three Portuguese sailors were shipwrecked on a remote southern island. Portuguese and Spanish missionaries soon arrived in Japan and at first Christianity made great headway, but the authorities' attitude towards the foreign religion was always unpredictable. Hideyoshi was alternately friendly and hostile, and there were increasingly severe persecutions under the second and third Tokugawa shoguns, culminating in the 1637 Shimabara Rebellion which ended with the massacre of tens of thousands of believers. At the same time, early enthusiasm for secular, commercial contact with the outside world waned as the government became fearful of the threat of foreign conquest. A series of edicts prohibiting Japanese people from going abroad on pain of death, and confining Chinese traders to the southern port of Nagasaki, was followed in 1641 by the move of the Dutch trading post from Hirado, another southern port, to a small artificial island called Deshima, also in Nagasaki. From 1641 until 1854 China, Korea, the Ryukyu Islands (modern Okinawa Prefecture), and the Netherlands were the only foreign territories in regular contact with Japan. In the early years of *sakoku*, "national seclusion," there was a thriving export trade in Japanese porcelain, manufactured in the southern island of Kyushu using technical know-how brought back by prisoners-of-war captured during the Korean invasion. Because of political disruption in China, Japan was able to capture a significant percentage of the export market to Europe until the Chinese took over again towards the end of the seventeenth century. The same thing happened, on a smaller scale, in the case of lacquer.

Despite the limited nature of foreign trade, the picture of Edo-Period Japan as a culture almost entirely cut off from outside contact has been rejected by many recent scholars who stress that there was a high degree of awareness of world events. So, for example, Western technology was utilized and Western objects found homes not only among the ruling elite but also among the cultivated merchant classes of the great cities. Just as seventeenth- and eighteenth-century Japanese exports of porcelain and lacquer readied the West for a much larger influx of craft goods in the second half of the nineteenth century, so, too, did Japanese knowledge of Western medicine, optics, and military technology (mostly gathered from books written in Dutch) facilitate the country's rapid industrialization after the Meiji restoration. Although graphic art and painting fall outside the scope of this exhibition, it is worth noting that the Japanese print designers who were most popular in Europe and America during the early years of the Meiji Era, Hokusai and Hiroshige, were among the artists who had been most influenced by Western notions of perspective and shading during the supposed seclusion of the early nineteenth century. Nevertheless, it would be misleading to suggest that Edo-Period Japan was a truly international country. Aside from the special case of porcelain and lacquer, the crafts mostly followed an autonomous line of development, assisted by Tokugawa Ieyasu's success in establishing a system which maintained peace and security and prevented a return to civil war.

ECONOMIC PROBLEMS AND THE DECLINE OF THE SHOGUNATE

Prolonged peace, economic growth, and the bureaucratization of the samurai class, who were turned from warriors into officials or in some cases even lost their stipends altogether, turned the *shi-no-ko-sho* system (above) of the Tokugawa *bakufu* almost on its head. In terms of actual wealth rather than formal rank, the new urban merchant class came first, dominating much of the economy. As a result of the combination of the *sankin kotai* system (above) with a flourishing market economy, Edo in the eighteenth century (when Japan had a population of about thirty million) was, as we have already seen, the largest city in the world, with more than a million residents, half of them members of the samurai class and the other half people who supplied goods and services needed by the whole population, including high-quality craft goods. Both Kyoto and Osaka are thought to have had populations of around 600,000, the former continuing to thrive as a center of the arts and the latter developing into a great merchant city and the hub of the trade in rice, *sake*, soya beans, and other essentials. Thanks to the combined patronage of *daimyo*, merchants and urban samurai who had adopted merchant ways, metalwork, lacquer, ceramics, textiles, and carving flourished as never before.

Despite the growing prosperity of the cities and a more modest increase in living standards in the countryside, frequent disasters such as earthquakes, tidal waves, fires–an estimated 100,000 lives were lost, for example, in the great fire of Edo in 1657–and famines (which killed far more people) made for increasing social instability and tension between rich and poor and town and country. Periods of inflation in the price of necessities, particularly rice which served as the main measure of wealth in much the same way as the dollar in today's world economy, made life difficult for everyone except the richest merchants. These economic crises were particularly wounding to the esteem of middle-ranking and junior samurai who depended on fixed incomes. The shogunate tried to arrest its declining economic power through a series of bungled reforms, but by the time of the devastating Tempo famine which ran from 1833 to 1838 a sense of national decay, coupled with an awareness of the growing threat from the great European powers, led many senior members of the elite to question the regime's ability to cope. The Japanese were well aware of the might of Russia (which had tried to establish contact a generation earlier) and France, and knew that Britain had easily defeated once-mighty China in First Opium War of 1842. They also had occasional contacts with the United States, thanks to the expansion of the New England whaling industry into the North Pacific. In 1837, for example, the *U.S.S. Morrison* unsuccessfully tried to land Japanese castaways near Edo, and in 1841 a young Japanese whaler, John Manjiro, was rescued by an American ship, eventually reaching New Bedford, Massachusetts (he did not return to Japan until 1851).

THE ARRIVAL OF COMMODORE PERRY AND THE OPENING UP OF JAPAN

From an American point of view, the opening of Japan can be seen as part of the young nation's rapid westward expansion in the decades before the Civil War. The advance to the Oregon Territory, the accession of California and Texas to the Union, and the growth of the whaling industry all drew American attention towards East Asia. From a Japanese standpoint, the United States did not appear to be a predatory Great Power in the same way as Russia or Great Britain; like Japan it was a comparative newcomer to the world of geopolitics. Following unsuccessful diplomatic missions to Japan in 1846 and 1849, the largest United States fleet ever seen in the Pacific arrived off Uraga at the southern end of present-day Tokyo Bay on July 8, 1853, under the command of Commodore Matthew Perry with orders from President Fillmore not to tolerate insults or slights of any kind. Perry's ships waited for several days while the shogunate decided how to respond. Finally, Perry was ordered to go to Nagasaki, the only port officially open to trade with Western countries. However, this response had been anticipated in Washington, and Perry was under instructions not to agree to it. On July 14, Perry and some of his officers and men were allowed to land long enough to hand over a letter from the President requesting proper treatment of shipwrecked seamen, ports of refuge where ships could obtain coal and stores, and the opening of trade. Perry added a more strongly worded letter of his own stating that if his "very reasonable and pacific overtures" were not at once accepted, he would have to return for a reply the following spring, "with a much larger force."

While Perry's squadron steamed off for a tour of South-East Asian ports, the Japanese struggled to reach a decision on the best way to deal with his proposition. Tokugawa Nariaki, the leader of a powerful branch of the ruling family, suggested a call to arms and limited importation of Western weapons until the country was in a position to respond with military force. Nariaki also suggested that it might be necessary to restore the power of the emperor in order to deal with the situation, a recommendation that heralded the events of the late 1860s. Abe Masahiro, a senior councilor, took the unusual step of consulting with the *daimyo*. Most of them rejected the idea of acceding to the President Fillmore's request, citing the time-honored nature of the seclusion policy, the dangers of Christianity and China's recent experience at the hands of the British, but a few of them conceded that Japan was too weak to have much choice in the matter. The sudden death of the shogun Ieyoshi in August heightened the sense of crisis, and a decree on December 1, 1853, eventually suggested that since Japan's defenses were inadequate Perry should be given no clear answer; if he used force, however, Japan must do what it could to defend itself.

On February 13 the following year, Perry returned and it soon became clear to the Japanese authorities that he would not be satisfied by a vague response. A formal meeting and exchange of papers between Commodore Perry and the Japanese side took place on March 8 at Kanagawa, a village near Yokohama at the mouth of Edo Bay, and on the last day of the month the Treaty of Kanagawa was signed. The opening paragraph of the Treaty declared that:

> There shall be a perfect, permanent and universal peace, and a
> sincere and cordial amity, between the United States of America
> on the one part, and the Empire of Japan on the other, and between
> their people, respectively, without exception of persons or places ...

Under the Treaty's other terms, the ports of Shimoda and Hakodate were opened as ports of refuge and it was agreed to appoint consuls at a later date. The Treaty did not, however, give specific permission for trade. Although the concessions exacted by Perry, as well as similar deals concluded soon afterwards by the Russians and the British, failed to satisfy mercantile opinion in Europe and America, they were the first step in a process that would quickly build up an unstoppable momentum.

Just as important as the exact content of the Treaty of Kanagawa was the symbolism and pageantry of the meeting between the two nations. Perry was keenly aware of the importance of ceremonial and fully understood the significance of the Japanese rituals of formal entertainment and gift exchange. Authorized to spend the then enormous sum of $20,000 to buy presents for the "emperor" (Perry and his staff were hazy about the respective roles of shogun and emperor), Perry brought with him such treasures as a complete set of John James Audubon's *Birds of America* and *Quadrupeds of North America*–these lavish publications were valued at an astronomical $1,000 each. There was also a case of firearms made by Samuel Colt, a daguerreotype camera, and a telegraph machine from Samuel Morse, the inventor of the code which bears his name. Most impressive of all, however, was a quarter-scale locomotive which ran on a 350-foot circle on a narrow-gauge track. The Japanese delegation lined up for hours to take a ride and:

> as they were unable to reduce themselves to the capacity of the
> carriage ... they betook themselves to the roof and, clinging to its
> edge, went whirling round, their robes flapping in the breeze,
> grinning with intense interest.

The gifts Perry received in return included:

> ... specimens of rich brocades and silks, of their famous lacquered
> ware, such as chow-chow boxes, tables, trays, and goblets, all
> skillfully wrought and finished with an exquisite polish; of porcelain
> cups of wonderful lightness and transparency, adorned with figures
> and flowers in gold and variegated colors, and exhibiting a workmanship
> which surpassed even that of the ware for which the Chinese are
> remarkable. Fans, pipe cases, and articles of apparel in ordinary use,
> of no great value but of exceeding interest, were scattered in among
> the more luxurious and costly objects.

This enthusiastic description was written by Francis L. Hawks, author of a narrative of the expedition, but one of his less open-minded fellow-officers, Edward Yorke McCauley, was unimpressed, recording in his diary that the Japanese presents were "nothing very remarkable, or which could not be produced superior in the U.S." The next fifty years were to demonstrate that despite McCauley's scepticism, the skills of Japan's lacquerers, metalworkers, potters and enamelers would find a ready market in the United States.

CHAPTER THREE

REVOLUTIONS AND EXHIBITIONS: FROM PERRY TO THE CENTENNIAL

THE MEIJI RESTORATION

The sequence of diplomatic and political developments leading from the Treaty of Kanagawa to the Meiji Restoration of 1868 was extremely complex. The aim of the Western powers, led first by the United States and later, with the outbreak of the American Civil War, by Great Britain and France, was to open Japan to trade. Once the Japanese had realized that Western military might made it impossible to carry on with the policy of seclusion, the leadership was roughly divided into two factions. The conservatives advocated minimal concessions and minimal changes to the existing political system in the hope of an eventual return to the old ways. The reformers, mainly senior samurai from the west of the country, wanted a radical reform of government and society so that Japan could protect herself, compete with her foreign rivals, and change the terms of treaties she had signed under indirect threat of military force.

After the conclusion of the first, tentative treaties, the United States, in the person of its first Consul-General, Townsend Harris, pushed ahead with plans for more substantial agreements. To that end, he submitted a Treaty of Amity and Commerce in early 1858 under which a further six ports, including Edo and Osaka, would be opened to foreign trade between 1859 and 1863. The Japanese authorities hesitated, but news of Britain and France's victory over China in the "Arrow" War and their plans to send an expedition to Japan at last forced them to sign, although the treaty was described as "a blemish on our Empire and a stain on our divine land." It was followed by similar agreements with Britain, France, the Netherlands, and Russia. Under the provisions of these "unequal treaties," Westerners in Japan enjoyed extraterritorial rights and were not subject to the laws of Japan, but Japanese residents abroad received no such privileges in return. In an effort to lessen the effects of the concessions they had already made, the Japanese demanded that facilities for trade should be built at the fishing village of Yokohama instead of at nearby Kanagawa as laid down in the treaties. This move would, it was thought, cut the foreign community off from the main Edo-Kyoto-Osaka road and make it easier to control its activities. Western diplomats agreed under protest but the new town quickly grew and prospered, becoming the focal point of Japan's foreign relations and the center of its trade. Many of the works of art on view in this exhibition would have left Japan via Yokohama, and quite a few of them were manufactured there as well. Yokohama was a dangerous place in the early years. From 1859 there was a series of attacks by junior samurai on Western officials and traders in both Yokohama and Edo, and their nationalist anger was not directed solely against foreigners: on March 24, 1860, Ii Naosuke, a senior government figure and architect of Japan's response to the second wave of treaties, was cut down outside Edo Castle.

For a short time the United States and Britain offered to tone down the treaties in an effort to shore up the shogunate and pacify its opponents, but further murders in 1862 caused a hardening of British attitudes. Twelve British warships were assembled at Yokohama to support demands for an indemnity of 100,000 pounds sterling, and a full apology from Satsuma, a domain in the far south of Japan whose soldiers had killed a British subject. In 1863 the forces of Choshu, a domain in the western part of Honshu Island, fired on American, Dutch, and French ships, inflicting casualties and effectively closing the strategic Straits of Shimonoseki to foreign shipping. Shortly afterwards, the British navy sustained heavy damage when it bombarded the town of Kagoshima, capital of Satsuma. These partial successes encouraged some samurai to believe that Japan was already strong enough to repel the foreigners, but in September 1864 a multinational force of seventeen ships bombarded the Choshu batteries and put men ashore to dismantle the military installations.

The shogunate at last agreed to pay an indemnity of three million dollars and, despite desperate efforts by lesser samurai to bring down the regime, the focus of opposition moved from conservative fanatics to moderate realists. As the great statesman Ito Hirobumi put it on his return from a visit to Great Britain in 1865:

> ... so-called irrational extremists have for the most part had their
> eyes opened so that they have come to argue the impossibility of
> expulsion and even recommend the opening of the country.

An alliance of three powerful domains, Satsuma, Choshu, and Tosa, whose views were shared by some figures within the administration, culminated towards the end of 1867 in a *coup d'état*, and a brief civil war that brought down the Tokugawa shogunate and marked the end of the Tokugawa or Edo Period. Much of the opposition to the Tokugawa had been carried out in the imperial name, and the death in 1867 of the Emperor Komei gave the leaders of the reform faction the opportunity to enlist the tacit support of his fifteen-year-old successor, who moved from Kyoto to Tokyo, the new capital, in 1868. However, although the events of 1867–68 are called the "Meiji Restoration," this does not mean that the emperor actually wielded executive power. Just as in previous centuries, the small and powerful oligarchy that would oversee the most sweeping changes in the country's history based its authority on the fact that it ruled with his consent. His role remained ceremonial, but became more public. As well as performing the ancient court rituals, he received visiting dignitaries, opened exhibitions and railways, and presided at solemn state occasions such as the announcement of the new constitution in 1889.

JAPAN REFORMS AND THE WEST TAKES NOTICE

During the decade from 1867 to 1877, the new Japanese government's chief priorities were the consolidation of its power, the introduction of basic reforms, and the rapid development of Western technology. It is a tribute to the Meiji leaders' determination and keen commercial sense that, despite these urgent tasks, the same period also marks the beginning of the "Japanese Craze" that would sweep Europe and America in the last quarter of the nineteenth century. By 1877, when a rebellion led by a conservative samurai, Saigo Takamori, was successfully put down by the new conscript army, the Meiji government had found the time and resources to participate successfully in two international expositions and mount a major domestic exposition of its own. Already in the 1850s and 1860s the pace of technological and institutional innovation had quickened. The *daimyo* of Satsuma appointed Western experts to help with his industrialization plans and even the conservative shogunate set up a translation bureau. This willingness to reform meant that as early as 1858 a British diplomat could note that, compared to backward China, "the Japanese, if not actually in a state of progressive advancement, are in a condition to profit by the flood of light that is about to be poured in upon them." The urgent sense of the need to learn as much as possible from the West was evident in the decision to send what would now be called fact-finding missions to America and Europe in 1860 and 1861. The Japanese delegation to the U.S. visited several cities and was seen on Broadway by Walt Whitman, who wrote these verses in *The New York Times*:

> Over the Western sea hither from Niphon come,
> Courteous, the swart-cheek'd two-sworded envoys,
> Leaning back in their open barouches, bare-headed impassive,
> Ride to-day through Manhattan ...
>
> My sail-ships and steam-ships threading the archipelagoes
> My stars and stripes fluttering in the wind
> Commerce opening, the sleep of ages having done its work, races
>   reborn, refresh'd,
> Lives, works resumed–the object I know not–but the old, the Asiatic
>   renew'd as it must be,
> Commencing from this day surrounded by the world.

By 1872, things were changing so fast that the American teacher William Griffis, back from only a year in the provinces, enthused:

> Tokyo is so modernized that I scarcely recognize it ... No beggars, no
> guardhouses, no sentinels ... no swords worn ... new decencies and
> proprieties observed; lesscuticle visible; more clothes. The age of pantaloon
> has come. Thousands wearing hats, boots, coats; carriages numerous; jin-riki-shas
> countless. Shops full of foreign wares and notions. Soldiers all uniformed, armed
> with ... rifles. New bridges span the canals. Police in uniform. Hospitals, schools
> and colleges ... Railway nearly finished ... Old Yedo [Edo] has passed away
> forever. Tokyo, the national capital is a cosmopolis.

Griffis's words aptly sum up the keynotes of those early years: industrialization, abolition of old institutions and their replacement by Western equivalents, and a craze for the outward aspects of Western fashion and manners. Speed is the most striking aspect of all the reforms. In the four years to the end of 1872 the old feudal domains had been abolished, systems of national primary education and military service had been announced, telegraphs were in widespread use in the capital region, the railway between Tokyo and Yokohama was completed, and the first government-sponsored exhibition was held in a Tokyo temple. The envoys sent to Europe ten years earlier were probably the first to become aware of the growing importance there of both museums and international expositions, and that a few Japanese items had even made their way into Western public collections. It was not until 1862, however, that the groundwork for what would become the Japanese Craze was laid by the British diplomat Sir Rutherford Alcock, an assertive and independent-minded figure who is also said to have been the first Westerner to climb Mount Fuji. Alcock's Japanese display for the London International Exhibition in 1862 included nearly a thousand objects, providing an introduction to Japanese art for more than six million visitors. By this date the great government-sponsored exhibition had become a familiar feature of international commercial and cultural life. The epoch-making 1851 Great Exhibition at the Crystal Palace in London was soon imitated in many countries. Americans erected their own (not very successful) Crystal Palace in New York City in 1853–4, and there were similar events in Dublin (1853), Munich (1854), and Paris (1855). Later, instead of being held in a single large building, fairs spread over many acres and included great halls devoted to such topics as agriculture, education, electricity, gardening, "liberal arts," machinery, transportation, and even crime and punishment. Typically they took place in specially constructed buildings (which sometimes outlasted the exhibitions they held by only a few months), included outdoor as well as indoor displays, and were enlivened by a host of extra attractions such as "native villages," "pleasances," "pikes," bazaars, and fairgrounds. The numbers attending them were huge (fifty million at the 1900 Paris exposition) and they often covered a vast area. In the years after the American Civil War, Philadelphia (1876), Chicago (1893), and St. Louis (1904) were to host some of the greatest expositions ever held.

JAPAN AT THE WORLD EXPOSITIONS

The fact that Japan's emergence on the world stage coincided with the development of this new means of truly global communication gave the Meiji leaders a powerful incentive to ensure that their country was fully represented at every major show. Japan had in fact participated in two major exhibitions even before the Meiji Era, once as we have already seen in 1862 and again in 1867 when both the shogunate (which showed more than 1,300 items) and its enemies in Satsuma and Saga (another part of Kyushu Island) organized rival displays at the Paris exhibition, causing the event's director to ask despairingly, "Who are the *real* Japanese?" The Meiji government's first formal participation in a world exhibition took place at Vienna in 1873. Although a number of factors, in particular the international banking crisis of 1872, made the Vienna World Exhibition a financial disaster, it was still an enormous event, and one of the first to follow the example of the 1872 Moscow Polytechnic Exhibition in setting up separate halls for Machinery, Fine Art, and Agriculture. It covered every aspect of contemporary science, art, and technology, and attempted to outdo anything accomplished in

London or Paris over the preceding twenty years. For example, the Paris exhibition of 1867 had featured a large scale model of the Suez Canal (opened in 1869), complete with ships passing through it. Not to be outdone, the Vienna display included a model of the entrance to the Mont Cenis Tunnel between Italy and France, with railroad track, signaling, and train. As the official British report commented:

> It may well be doubted whether the practical and the picturesque, the modern
> and the medieval, the East and the West, will ever again mingle in one
> harmonious whole ... as on the Prater of 1873, in the Buildings on the Park.

All of this presented an unmissable opportunity for research and study, and one of the multifarious aims of the Iwakura mission, a high-level Japanese group that traveled in North America and Europe from 1871 to 1873, was to visit the exposition and see what lessons their country could learn from the achievements of the West. As a member of the mission wrote:

> ... if the country is to be enriched, the army strengthened, and
> education established, then first production must be encouraged
> among the people, products of every kind manufactured and
> exported overseas, goods imported that our country lacks ...

On its return, the Iwakura delegation produced a massive report which provided Japan with much of the information it needed in order to become a fully industrialized nation.

For its own display at Vienna the Japanese government allotted 500,000 yen from its limited national resources (this was 0.8 percent of the entire national expenditure for 1873), and entrusted much of the policy-making to a German, Gottfried Wagener, who was teaching chemistry in Japan as one of many foreign specialists invited by the government. In view of Japan's low level of industrial development, he decided that the Japanese displays should center not on canals or railroads but on technically refined decorative arts, thus appealing to a taste for exotic goods already kindled by the displays of 1862 and 1867. Both at Vienna and at later exhibitions, Japan's success was the result of centralized organization, meticulous preparation, and early recognition of the need to cater to Western interests. Even more important, the very lack of modern industrial products made the government focus on the decorative arts in exhibitions and other forms of trade promotion, so much so that they accounted for about one-tenth of total national exports from the late 1870s until the early 1890s. Considering that the great majority of such goods were made entirely by hand, this is an extraordinarily high figure. Even as late as 1904, when the country had developed a modern industrial sector as well as vastly increasing its production and export of copper, raw silk, and tea, the displays at St. Louis were still dominated by hand-produced craft goods. From 1870 to 1910, government sponsorship, coupled on occasion with the patronage of the emperor and his family, provided leading craftspeople with an almost ideal environment in which to refine the skills they had inherited from their Edo-Period forbears, and made it possible for them to produce the works, of a technical excellence not seen before or since, that are the subject of this exhibition and catalogue.

By insisting on the highest standards, the authorities ensured that the Japanese displays were always among the most highly praised, but it was also determined to see that this praise was turned to commercial advantage. Because there was no other organization in the early Meiji Era capable of taking on the role, the central government played an unusually direct part in the promotion of crafts for export after the Vienna exhibition was over by setting up a semi-public trading company, the Kiritsu Kosho Kaisha. The initiative for this promising move came from Sano Tsunetami, a leading reformer and the vice-president of the Japanese Exhibition Bureau at Vienna, but day-to-day management was entrusted to a tea merchant, Matsuo Gisuke, and an art dealer, Wakai Kenzaburo. These two expanded the business by acting as representatives of the government and complementing the national displays at international exhibitions, a unique position which soon resulted in their opening overseas branches in New York (1876) and Paris (1878). After a good start, Kiritsu Kosho Kaisha later got into financial difficulties since exhibitions were organized on political as much as commercial grounds and it was often forced to display products which were so expensive as to be unsalable. Before it was eventually forced to close down in 1891, however, it exerted a strong influence on the overall direction of wares made for export, commissioning more than 2,000 preliminary drawings, employing many of the leading potters, lacquerers, embroiderers, and enamelers of the day and buying a comprehensive range of ready-made products from other artists. After 1891, the Kiritsu Kosho Kaisha's role was taken over by other, purely commercial, companies which had sprung up in the 1870s and 1880s. The government also sought to maintain high standards at the exhibitions by directly commissioning a further 2,500 design sketches in preparation for the 1876 Centennial Exhibition at Philadelphia, the first and second Domestic Expositions in 1877 and 1881, and the 1878 Paris Exhibition.

THE PHILADELPHIA CENTENNIAL: AMERICA SALUTES JAPAN

Japan's preparations for Vienna had been hurried. An official commission was not appointed until June 1872, barely one year before the fair opened and, although some magnificent pieces were eventually displayed and several prizes were won, this did not allow enough time for the elaborate planning that was necessary if Japan was to make a lasting impact on the international public. Japanese involvement at America's first great exposition, the Centennial Exhibition held at Philadelphia in 1876, was a very different matter, reflecting the superior organization of the entire event. Herman Joseph Schwarzmann, the twenty-seven-year old engineer who was responsible for the planning and layout of the exhibition grounds as well as the design of the Art Building, created the first properly landscaped and planned international exhibition at Philadelphia, paying meticulous attention to all the practical details taken for granted at comparable events today. The first concrete proposal for a centennial celebration was made in 1866 and planning for the festival began in March 1871, when Congress passed an act establishing the United States Centennial Commission, followed in 1872 by a Centennial Board of Finance to manage the budget. In 1874 officials were appointed and construction began on a site in Fairmount Park by the Schuylkill River. The exhibition would cover some 236 acres and include around 250 buildings, some of them quite small but others among the largest in the world–the Main Building was 1,880 feet long by 464 feet wide.

The Japanese learned about the centennial celebration as early as June 1873 and decided to participate in 1874, committing $600,000 to the event, the largest sum invested by any of the thirty participating nations. Okubo Toshimichi, a member of the Iwakura mission and, from 1873, Minister for Home Affairs, set up a Centennial Office and made his priorities clear by putting it under the control of a new Board of Commerce, Trade, and Agriculture. Once again, foreign help was enlisted in commissioning and selecting the exhibits, but this time the range of advisors was wider, including an Englishman and an American in addition to Gottfried Wagener. In July 1875 a special envoy, Sekizawa Akeo, arrived in Philadelphia to take charge of the local office and immediately set about achieving his superiors' three main objectives. These were to ensure that they could arrange the exhibits as they wished, get much more space for them, and be allowed to sell them afterwards. Sekizawa was extremely successful in the inevitable battle for space, eventually securing 17,831 square feet, an impressive increase on the 7,290 originally offered. This extra floor area was certainly going to be needed, since up to 30,000 items were gathered from all over Japan. The total freight, shipped to San Francisco and then carried free of charge by the Central Pacific Railroad Co., was estimated at 1,300 tons. In addition, the Japanese erected a Japanese dwelling for their high officials and, in a pattern repeated at many international arts events down to the present, the workmen sent to build the structure, with their dark blue uniforms, unfamiliar tools, deadpan expressions, and manual dexterity, excited widespread comment and served as an excellent curtain-raiser to the main event. Such crowds gathered to watch the strange, "almond-eyed" carpenters at work that a special fence had to be erected to protect them.

Although the presence of the Emperor of Brazil meant that the Japanese delegation was rather overshadowed on the opening day, May 10, the size and splendor of the Japanese exhibit made a deep impression on visitors and press alike. The display, overhung with large Japanese flags and long banners decorated with the imperial chrysanthemum crest, was arranged on two diagonal platforms with a one-hundred-foot frontage. The entrance was flanked by two elaborate five-foot high bronzes and, as at Vienna, bronzes were prominent elsewhere in the exhibit, visitors mentioning in particular a vase surmounted by an eagle with flights of birds forming its handles, as well as bronze cranes, tortoises, hens, and rabbits. One of the centerpieces was a formidable display of ceramics arranged on a wedding-cake-like stand twelve feet high, with examples from many of the main Japanese kilns, ranging in size from huge Arita porcelain vases to tiny tea cups. Other cases were filled to bursting with lacquer, ivory, and more metalwork. According to one commentator, the Japanese exhibit was:

> ... one of the great surprises of the fair ... We have been accustomed to
> regard that country as uncivilized, or half-civilized at the best, but we found
> here abundant evidences that it outshines the most cultivated nations of
> Europe in arts which are their pride and glory, and which are regarded as
> among the proudest tokens of their high civilization.

More condescendingly but no less admiringly, another visitor wondered:

> The quaint little people with their shambling gait, their eyes set awry in
> their head, and their grave and gentle ways, how can it be in them ...
> to make such wonderful things?

After studying the Japanese display, visitors could shop in the Japanese bazaar just north of the Main Building. Like the Japanese residence, this had been constructed by Japanese workmen and it included the first Japanese garden in America, complete with pines, camellias, stone lanterns, a stream, and a bamboo fence. The bazaar itself was an open pavilion and the stalls, run by ordinary Japanese merchants and their families, were stacked with ivories, fans, lanterns, screens, bronze figures, lacquers, toys, pottery, and bamboo, mostly of inferior quality to the pieces in the main display, but still extremely popular. Although some commentators criticized the over-commercial attitude of the Japanese, these items, together with the rest of the exhibits that went on sale after the Centennial closed, at much higher prices, started a craze for Japanese artifacts that would last for three decades.

Although many nations took part in the Centennial, Japan stood out sharply and unexpectedly from the rest. This was partly because of the Meiji government's commitment in manpower and resources. Only Great Britain shipped more material to the event, few participants secured more space than Japan in the Main Building, and Japan was one of only nine countries to erect a separate national residence for its officials. But perhaps an even more important reason for Japan's success was the fact that this was, for most Americans, their first contact with Japanese culture. The ten million visitors to Philadelphia in 1876 were highly impressed by the novelty of the Japanese displays and fascinated by the contrast between Japanese design and the predominantly High Victorian style of the European stands. Comparing the masterpieces of European medieval art with the Japanese antiquities on show, one writer criticized the former's "clumsiness of design and execution" and praised the latter's "grace and elegance of design and fabulous perfection of workmanship." Japan also appealed to America for the same reason that had made Commodore Perry the right man to open up the country twenty-three years earlier: both nations were new to the international scene and felt that they could deal with each other on equal terms. Another facet of American interest in Japan was shared with European Japanophiles. While they could admire the antiquity, real or apparent, of much that was put on view and envy Japan's imagined freedom from the ravages of the Industrial Revolution, they were also aware that her society and culture were changing at a tremendous rate. The tension between tradition and modernity was a continuing source of fascination. The officials who planned Japan's participation at later exhibitions were aware of this fascination, and did all they could to ensure that their displays both satisfied the Western love of exoticism and showed that their country was abreast of contemporary international taste.

CHAPTER FOUR

THE GOLDEN AGE OF MEIJI DECORATION: FROM PHILADELPHIA TO PARIS, 1876–1900

THE NATIONAL INDUSTRIAL EXPOSITIONS

Following its success at Philadelphia, Japan took part in many of the international exhibitions that followed: Paris in 1878, 1889, and 1900, Amsterdam in 1883, New Orleans and Nuremburg in 1885, Barcelona in 1887, Chicago in 1893, St. Louis in 1904, and London in 1910. In addition, a total of five Naikoku Kangyo Hakurankai [National Industrial Expositions] were held in Japan: the first (1877), second (1881), and third (1890) in Tokyo, the fourth (1895) in Kyoto, and the fifth (1903) in Osaka, followed by a Kangyo Hakurankai [Industrial Exhibition] in Tokyo in 1907. These events in Japan were organized at irregular intervals to avoid clashes with the great world exhibitions, for which they served as a kind of testing ground, and their division of displays followed the international format, in particular its evolving distinction between "fine art" and "industrial art" or "art manufacture." The Industrial Expositions were an integral part of the government's project to consolidate its power and press ahead with a program of industrialization and radical social and economic reform. As nationwide events, they nt only promoted competition by offering prizes to the most enterprising and innovative exhibitors, but also helped to foster a sense of shared Japanese national identity–something that had been largely absent during the Edo Period with its system of devolved feudal government and local loyalties. They were also among the earliest mass events of Japan's modern age. Even though there was no national transportation system, 454,168 people managed to attend during the three months of the first National Industrial Exposition, and 823,094 during the four-month run of the second Exposition.

Private enterprises like the Ozeki Company also promoted craft goods to foreign visitors, and they were equally active at exhibitions at home and abroad, participating fully in a symbiotic relationship with government, which assisted their efforts by publishing design manuals and preparing detailed reports before and after each major event. These reports provided advice on the motifs that would find favor abroad, and the shapes and sizes that were most appropriate to Western interiors, while the carefully recorded remarks of the prize judges gave aesthetic guidance and noted, with approval or disapproval, emerging trends in design and technique. Once it became clear to administrators and entrepreneurs alike that it was the very "Japaneseness" of Japanese art and craft that made it so salable, the strongly Westernizing trends of the 1870s and 1880s were gradually reversed, and the government began to take active steps to promote traditional art-forms and find ways of adapting them to contemporary market conditions. This development was due in part to the influence of Ernest Fenollosa, a Harvard graduate who taught philosophy for eight years in the Imperial University. Leading craftsmen in metal and lacquer were commissioned to make copies of famous old pieces unearthed from the collections of Buddhist temples and Shinto shrines, an Imperial Museum was established in 1889, and the Tokyo Art School (later renamed Tokyo University of Arts) opened in 1887. Under the leadership of Fenollosa's pupil Okakura Tenshin, who was named principal of the School in 1890, it pursued a Japanizing agenda that also guided the officials who were in charge of the selection of exhibits for the 1893 Columbian World's Fair, held in Chicago.

THE CHICAGO FAIR

As the four-hundredth anniversary of the discovery of America in 1492 drew near, there was a lot of discussion in the American press and in Congress as to how it could best be commemorated. It was finally decided that another great international exposition should be held, and by summer 1889 New

York, Washington, St. Louis, and Chicago had all established committees to press their claims. In April 1890 Congress passed an act selecting Chicago for the site, but it was already clear that the project could not be completed in time for the anniversary year. The Columbian World's Fair or World's Columbian Exposition finally opened on May 1, 1893 and ran until October 31, although a formal dedication ceremony was held in late 1892 to preserve the historical justification for the event.

The Chicago Fair was the last and the greatest of the nineteenth century's international expositions (if 1900, when the great Paris Exposition Universelle was held, is taken as the first year of the twentieth century). It covered 688 acres in Jackson Park on Lake Michigan, and attracted 27,539,000 visitors–almost a quarter of the total number of people then living in the United States. On its busiest day, October 9 or "Chicago Day," 716,881 went through the turnstiles. Almost in defiance of the considerable social turmoil of the early 1890s–and a devastating depression in 1893 itself–the Fair was a supremely optimistic event, and everything about it was on a grand scale. The Manufactures and Liberal Arts Building, for example, covered over eleven acres of exhibition space and rose to a height of 212 feet, reachable by giant Otis elevators which took visitors up to the flat roof to gaze out over the vast site. The official pavilions, with their celebration of industry, commerce, and technology, were supplemented by the attractions of the "Midway Pleasance," with a host of "native villages" and bazaars from around the world, including Japan, as well as fixed observation balloons ($2 per ascent), and a giant wheel 250 feet in diameter built by a Mr. G. W. G. Ferris of Pittsburg which could carry 2,160 people at a time in 36 cars.

"The White City"

Despite, or perhaps because of, Chicago's reputation as a brash go-ahead city, already in 1890 the site of the first skyscrapers designed by Louis Sullivan, the buildings of the fair were designed in a conservative style that was officially called "Neo-classical Florentine" and unified by a gigantic architectural order with arches sixty feet high. Although the internal structures of the largest pavilions were industrial and utilitarian, reflecting the latest developments in iron and steel technology, they were completely disguised by exterior walls made from "staff," a malleable mixture of plaster, cement, and fiber. Powered sprayers–one of many inventions that owe their origin to the fair–were used to paint the buildings white to resemble marble, and at night they were lit by electricity, giving rise to the popular designation, "The White City," in contrast to "The Black City," a nickname previously applied to Chicago because of its industrial grime.

Sullivan, appalled by the historicist approach of the fair's principal architect, Daniel H. Burnham, and planner, Frederick Law Olmsted, wrote: "thus architecture died in the land of the free and the home of the brave ... the damage wrought by the World's Fair will last for half a century." But although Olmsted's giant colonnades, lagoons, arches, domes, and piazzas may seem to us an incongruous setting for an event that was, in essence, a celebration of everything modern and industrial–even futuristic–they made a tremendous impression on visitors. The many detailed photographs of the event, preserved in a host of guidebooks and albums, still convey something of the grandeur of the fair and its pivotal place in the development of American industry, commerce, and popular culture.

The Phoenix Palace

The exhibits sent by the Japanese to Chicago in 1893 are often seen as the apogee of the Meiji decorative style. By that date, twenty years of government and imperial patronage had enabled masters such as Miyagawa Kozan in porcelain, Yabu Meizan in earthenware, Namikawa Sosuke in enamel, and Suzuki Chokichi in bronze to improve on the techniques they had inherited from the Edo Period and take their art to hitherto undreamed levels of perfection. Just as at Philadelphia in 1876, the Japanese exhibits were among the most highly praised for the delicacy and finish of the metal and ivory work, the bronzes, the pottery, and the porcelain.

Following the promulgation of the Constitution in 1889, the Imperial Diet [congress] held its first session in March 1890, and even though no official invitation had yet been received, it proposed that provision should be made for Japanese participation in the Chicago Fair. In November the government formally applied to the Diet for 630,000 yen. This was passed by a unanimous vote, and six months later a Preliminary Exhibition Bureau was established in the Ministry of Agriculture and Commerce, with an advisory council made up of leading figures from industry and commerce. A network of related associations was set up throughout the country and the response was overwhelming: the government had originally expected to ship 1,000 tons of exhibits, three times the amount sent to the 1889 Paris Exposition, but the initial bids totaled 7,000 tons. Eventually this was reduced to a final figure of 1,750 tons, still more than five times the Philadelphia total.

Just as they did at Philadelphia, the Japanese authorities quickly set about obtaining as much display space as possible. Despite the size of the fair site, the American organizers found themselves under enormous pressure from competing claims of the participating nations. However, Japan succeeded once again in securing a generous settlement that included 40,000 square feet in the Manufactures and Liberal Arts Building, 2,850 square feet in the Palace of Fine Arts, and substantial spaces in the Educational, Women's, Horticultural, and several other major buildings, as well as 40,000 square feet on Wooded Island, a spit of land located in a lagoon near the United States Government Building. The intention had been for the island to be a haven of peace from the hubbub of the fair, but the Japanese were allowed to use it for the construction of the Ho-oden [Phoenix Palace], an adaptation of the eleventh-century Ho-odo [Phoenix Hall] at Uji, a town south of Kyoto. The change of name symbolized the fact that the architecture of the building had also been altered for didactic purposes, so that its three main components could give visitors an idea of the style of three different periods. The north wing was Fujiwara or Late Heian Period (980–1185), based on both the original building at Uji and the Imperial Palace in Kyoto, with rounded posts, hinged shutters and blinds, and a display of historic bronzes, arms, armor, lacquerware, and pottery. The south wing reflected the Ashikaga or Muromachi Period (1333–1568), and was based on the famous Ginkakuji [Silver Pavilion] in Kyoto, with square posts and sliding screens. The interior of the central hall was a reproduction of a seventeenth-century castle, with modern wall paintings by students from Tokyo Art School.

The land around the Phoenix Palace was landscaped and planted in Japanese style, although the effect of a pocket of Eastern understatement set in the heart of the bombastic neoclassicism of the rest of the fair may have been blunted by the presence on Wooded Island of the Hunter's Cabin, a monument to Davy Crockett and Daniel Boone! The Palace was presented to the City of Chicago and was one of the few structures to survive the fair by more than a few months (most were soon looted or burned down), but it too eventually succumbed to a fire and was demolished in 1946. During the half century that it survived, however, it had a significant influence on American architects, in particular Frank Lloyd Wright, who collaborated with Louis Sullivan on some of the buildings of the fair and began to work independently in 1893.

"A new order of things"

Although the exotic building on Wooded Island, the seventh largest national pavilion in the fair, was the most prominent Japanese contribution to the overall appearance of "The White City," many other aspects of Japanese life were displayed in addition to the main displays of modern arts and crafts in the Manufactures and Fine Arts Buildings. There were exhibits of gardening, rice, tea, tobacco, razors, safes, and buttons, as well as photographs of railroad lines and statistics on education, life insurance, and crime, with the aim of parading Japan's efforts to catch up with the advanced nations of the West.

Japan was the only Asian nation granted a place in the prestigious setting of the Palace of Fine Arts, and even managed to get the amount of space allotted to it doubled in the course of the fair. Because so many of the other Japanese displays were concerned with state-of-the-art industrial and social developments, care was taken to ensure that the exhibits selected for this honor were of the very highest quality and could be easily distinguished from the more commercial wares on view elsewhere. The Japanese commissioners were aware that their paintings and sculptures were unlikely to make as great an impression on the American public as their porcelain, cloisonné enamel, textiles, and metalwork. As a result, they made a great effort to persuade their hosts that the three separate areas eventually given to Japan in the Palace of Fine Arts should be used in a completely different way from the spaces occupied in the same building by the U.S. and the European nations. A contemporary commentator noted that:

> Recognizing the radical differences between Japanese art and that
> of the western world, the authorities of the Art Department of the
> Columbian Exposition did not bind Japanese art exhibitors exclusively
> to the rigid classification established for other nations, but urged
> that the exhibit be made thoroughly national in character–exactly
> such an exhibit as would be formed under a classification devised
> for an art exhibition to be held in Japan.

If the official figures are to be believed, the effect of this concession was that no fewer than 270 of the 291 exhibits from all nations that gained admission to the Palace of Fine Arts, despite being defined as "decorative art," were Japanese. This is in complete contrast to the statistics for painting and sculpture, which show that only 24 out of 1,013 sculptures and 55 out of 7,357 paintings were Japanese. Although other records of the fair suggest slightly larger numbers of Japanese paintings and sculptures, there is no doubt that "works of decorative art" predominated in the Japanese display. Another commentator wrote that "the Japanese collection contained few pictures. It was largely made up of bronzes, carving in wood and ivory, lacquer, and embroideries." The distinction between the Art and the Industrial sections had become a significant issue in Japan as early as 1881 when, for example, the cloisonné enamels of Namikawa Sosuke were shown in the Art section at the second Naikoku Kangyo Hakurankai [National Industrial Exposition], while all other cloisonné artists who exhibited did so in the Industrial sections. The achievement of exhibition in the Art sections was perceived as mark of enhanced status and this must have made the selection process at Chicago an extremely delicate task, especially given the huge discrepancy in the spaces available: the area available in the Manufactures and Liberal Arts Building was fourteen times greater than that allotted in the Palace of Fine Arts. Another complicating factor was the dual purpose of the former building which, as its name implied, could include Remington typewriters and J. S. Bach's clavichord under the same roof!

Even the knowledgeable Captain Frank Brinkley, who saw the "Works of Art" (his phrase) selected for Chicago at a preview in Tokyo, was unable to predict the ultimate division of some of the exhibits. He was confident that the pair of colossal cloisonné enamel vases and censer submitted by Suzuki Shirozaemon would be excluded from the Palace of Fine Arts because "it is hard to wed politics with art," but in fact they were prominently displayed there under a canopy on the ground floor at the west end of the East Court, and singled out for attention by Hubert Howe Bancroft in his massive *Book of the Fair*:

> From Shirozayemon Suzuki come the three largest pieces of cloisonné
> that have ever been fashioned. Two of them are vases and the third
> an incense-burner, the former nearly nine feet high, designed for
> exhibition and costing more than two years of labor. Their figures
> of birds and animals are symbolic of the seasons and the virtues,
> and are also of national significance. On the top are red and white
> stripes inlaid with silver stars, with chrysanthemums and other floral
> devices emblematic of the friendship existing between Japan and
> the United States.

Despite all the problems, both methodological and diplomatic, faced by the Japanese commissioners, their selection of Japanese art succeeded in creating an overwhelmingly favorable impression. Among the most widely-praised exhibits was a wall hanging, measuring twenty by thirty feet, by Kawashima Jinbei of the annual festival at Nikko. According to Bancroft it "represented the two years' task of scores of weavers" and included more than 1,000 figures in the procession. It is still preserved in Chicago's Field Museum of Natural History. Brinkley correctly predicted that the Kawashima tapestry would be a hit with ordinary visitors to the fair; he was also right in thinking that their attention would be drawn by a famous set of twelve hawks from the atelier of Suzuki Chokichi that are now in the Imperial Collection. For the purposes of this catalogue, it is particularly interesting that a generalist like Bancroft should have been so struck not only by the huge cloisonné enamel vase, but also by two other pieces in the Khalili Collection that are almost certain to have been shown at Chicago. He mentions "Otake [Norikuni]'s bronze rooster, perched on a hollow stump, with a hen and chickens below, the feathers are wonderfully wrought, especially in the rooster's sweeping tail" as well as a porcelain vase by Miyagawa Kozan, "wave-patterned and with figures of dragons under the glaze," another work strongly commended by Brinkley.

Brinkley was especially pleased with the selection of ceramics, noting that only a few objects were included in the Fine Art section and that the rest, in particular the "Yokohama School," were relegated to the Manufactures Building–even though the division of the displays sometimes meant that leading artists exhibited in both buildings. Brinkley also praised the Japanese artists for their success in applying their skills to the creation of new types of product: "the talent is there, just as abundantly as ever, and the only perplexity is to find directions in which it can be usefully exercised." He was less encouraging about sculpture in wood, ivory, and cast metal, where he thought that "the exporters in the Settlements," (*i.e.* Yokohama, Kobe, and other ports) had "exercised a vitiating influence," but he did have some good words to say about Takamura Koun's horse-chestnut wood carving of a baboon, characteristically described incorrectly by Bancroft as a gorilla carved from cherrywood.

The Manufactures and Liberal Arts Building contained much larger and more commercial displays of Japanese porcelain, enamel, metalwork, textiles, and other media. Surviving photographs show row upon row of vast, densely packed vitrines, sometimes rather incongruously arranged beneath reconstructions of traditional Japanese architecture, but it is not easy to get a detailed idea of the kind of objects that were on view. Bancroft's description of the Japanese section in the Manufactures Building is confusing since he repeats, in different words, several of the descriptions that are included in his account of the Fine Arts. This suggests either that his vast series of volumes was actually the hastily-edited work of more than one writer, or that some of the exhibits were moved during the course of the fair. Nevertheless, he makes some general remarks that include a note of gentle criticism:

> The display is, however, less unique than at the Centennial Exposition,
> when ... a great demand was originated for Japanese articles, especially
> in the way of ornamentations ... As a result, the simple characteristics
> of earlier Japanese work have become somewhat vulgarized; for the
> restless commercial spirit has seized upon Japanese and American
> alike, and lowered the former standard. Nevertheless there are many
> specimens representing the purest results of Japanese handicraft ...

More popular accounts of the Fair, however, suggest that enthusiasm for Japanese "handicraft" was still growing rather diminishing:

> Appreciation of Japanese handicraft in decorative art is steadily increasing.
> The porcelains were nicely modeled and deftly painted ... The skill of native
> artificers was shown in metal engraving, lacquered ware, in wrought flowers
> and butterflies, toilet sets, fans, etc ... The wood and ivory carvings were of
> ingenious design and exquisite detail, as also the ceramic wares and mosaics.

The overall impact of Japan's participation in this great American event is perhaps best summed up in the following words:

> In the not very distant day when we shall receive envoys ... from
> the inhabitants of Mars ... to our own international expositions,
> these exhibits will probably not differ very much from our own
> than do those of the Empire of Japan in the present Chicago show ...
> The European or American who enters these galleries ... recognizes
> at once a new order of things and a new world ... [an] air of having
> come from somewhere beyond the stars.

Through careful management of the displays, the Japanese authorities had succeeded triumphantly in their aim of projecting their country as the repository of a culture that was uniquely distinct from that of the West. This success reflected the long-term policies of Kuki Ryuichi, who had visited the 1878 Paris Exposition as Vice-Minister of Education, and been impressed by the interest that was shown there in Japanese history and civilization. He returned home convinced that it was a mistake to promote Western art at the expense of traditional Japanese styles, as was increasingly happening at that time. In 1879 he was a member of the group of opinion-formers who set up the Ryuchikai, a society dedicated to the promotion of Japan's artistic heritage. In 1888 Kuki was named Director of the Imperial Museum, and in this capacity he served on several international and domestic exhibition committees. Due to his influence and that of Okakura Tenshin, Western art was at first excluded from the curriculum of the Tokyo Art School. However, in reaction to his policies, Japan's *yoga* artists–who painted in Western style using Western materials–boycotted both the third National Industrial Exposition in 1890 and the Chicago World's Fair.

As well as stressing the "Japaneseness" of Japan through their displays of art and craft, the organizers were anxious to prove in other parts of the fair that their country was "worthy of full fellowship in the family of nations," and could even, in the words of one American scholar, be "expected to have an uplifting–that is, Americanizing–influence on an otherwise backward Asian continent." While this public relations initiative helped to prepare international opinion for Japan's war with China in 1894–5, the conservative artistic policy of Kuki and his colleagues was challenged during the closing years of the nineteenth century.

THE PARIS EXPOSITION UNIVERSELLE

Both Kuki and his ally Okakura were ousted in the late 1890s and replaced by the Francophiles Hayashi Tadamasa and Kuroda Seiki. Hayashi and Kuroda believed that Western art had a major part to play in the development of Japanese culture. They ensured that Western painting was at last put on the curriculum of Tokyo Art School and also promoted the emergence of a type of naturalistic sculpture that depicted everyday Japanese subjects in a sometimes slightly sentimentalized Western style. Their influence on the decorative arts is seen in the redesignation of items submitted for exhibition at the vast Paris Exposition Universelle of 1900, an even more ambitious event than the 1893 World's Fair. The title of the category "Art Craft Object" was changed to "Craft Object of Excellence," and the entry regulations stipulated that crafts should be made on aesthetic principles, with both design and execution the responsibility of the maker, but these changes did not have a great effect on the actual appearance of the works sent to Paris. The French authorities made a much stricter distinction than the Americans between "Fine Arts"–painting, prints, sculpture, and architecture–and "Arts and Industrial Arts," a category which included decorative pieces that the Japanese had been allowed to show as Fine Arts at Chicago. This meant that Japanese ceramics and metalwork, for example, had to compete more directly with their Western counterparts, resulting in the Japanese displays being criticized as old- fashioned in comparison to the *art nouveau* style seen in the work of other advanced nations, even though *art nouveau* was in part the result of interaction between Japanese and Western styles. Japan's critical failure at Paris had a profound effect on Japanese crafts, and after 1900 there was a trend away from profuse decoration for its own sake towards greater integration of surface design and overall shape. Although the year 1900 has been chosen as a convenient point to conclude this chapter, this trend had actually surfaced a few years earlier in 1895, when the judges at the fourth National Industrial Exposition commented that an enamel by Namikawa Yasuyuki showed a shift from traditional motifs to "a picture far beyond a mere pattern." Again, in 1897, in a speech to the Yokohama Pottery Painting Association, Maeda Kasetsu said:

> … these days it seems fashionable to paint figures, landscapes, flowers,
> and birds inside a frame on a round vessel surface, and fill the
> outside of the frame with small designs. It destroys the shape of the
> vessel. Besides, it is too small to paint any pictures inside the frame.
> Even if it is possible to put some pictures inside, the small designs
> outside the frame obliterate the features inside and degrade the design.

Although this criticism did not immediately convince all of Japan's enamelers, potters, lacquerers, and metalworkers to change their ways, it did herald a general stylistic evolution that would make itself felt when Japan triumphed once again at the 1904 Louisiana Purchase Exposition.

CHAPTER FIVE

"THE YANKEES OF THE EAST": FROM PARIS TO LONDON, 1900–1910

MEET ME AT THE FAIR

The Paris Exposition of 1900 was the next major international show after the Columbian World's Fair, but a number of lesser events were held in the United States. These included the California Midwinter Exposition in San Francisco (1894), featuring a Japanese village built by an Australian-born American, and the ill-fated Pan-American Exposition (1901) held at Buffalo, New York. Intended partly as a celebration of the power of electricity drawn from the Niagara Falls hydroelectric scheme, the Exposition is notorious for the fact that President McKinley was shot there on September 6 at a reception in the Temple of Music and died eight days later. Aside from the assassination of the President, the most remembered aspect of the Buffalo Exposition was probably the "Midway" area which featured such spectacles as 700 representatives of the Indian Congress including Geronimo, who were put on display alongside the "Educated Horse" and "Chiquita, the Doll Lady." Similar side shows played an important part in many subsequent expositions, sometimes even eclipsing the main event.

Geronimo suffered the indignity of being exhibited again in 1904, this time at the much larger Louisiana Purchase Exhibition held in St. Louis. It was even bigger than the Chicago Fair; so huge, in fact, that all the exhibition buildings at Buffalo would have fit into the Palace of Agriculture which covered almost twenty acres. Once again the pavilions were faced with the mixture of plaster, cement, and fiber called "staff," and fashioned in the same ostentatious neoclassical manner as "The White City." This time, however, the style was more exuberant, and wood was used for the framework instead of iron and steel girders, giving the entire event an even greater air of impermanence. At the end of the fair, nearly all these temporary structures were pulled down; one exception being the building that now houses the St. Louis Art Museum. It is perhaps no accident that, by comparison with the Columbian World's Fair, the Louisiana Purchase Exhibition has left scant documentary evidence despite its ambitious scale. It was also less successful than its predecessor in attracting the crowds, with an attendance of about 19 million compared to Chicago's 27 million.

The official fair and the semi-official informal amusement area called the "Pike" included more than 1,500 buildings and covered 1,272 acres. A walk around the whole site would have covered thirty-five miles, including nine miles just to view the agricultural display. The Palace of Liberal Arts covered nine acres, with a giant auditorium seating more than 60,000 people, and the fair boasted a similar range of grandiose buildings to Chicago, arranged around a fan-shaped network of lagoons radiating from a Grand Basin with fountains spurting water seventy-five feet into the air. In addition to Liberal Arts, there were Palaces of Mines and Metallurgy, Manufactures, Education and Social Economy, Varied Industries, and Electricity. The entire site was constructed in less than three years despite 200 labor disputes. Although great efforts were made to emulate the more dignified aspects of the 1893 event, St. Louis is much better remembered for the glories of the Pike, the largest amusement area ever seen at an international exposition, and a precursor of the twentieth-century American tradition of mass outdoor entertainment, from Coney Island to Disneyworld. This light-hearted aspect of the fair was summed up in a famous song:

> Meet me in St. Louis, Louis,   We will dance the Hoochee-Koochee
> Meet me at the fair,   I will be your tootsie wootsie
> Don't tell me the lights are shining If you will meet me in St. Louis, Louis,
> Any place but there;   Meet me at the fair.

The largest attraction at the Pike was the Tyrolean Alps feature, complete with an Alpine village and inhabitants in native costume. It covered ten acres and was said to have cost $500,000. There were also a Magic Whirlpool, an Irish village, a reproduction ocean liner, recreations of street scenes from Cairo and Paris, and Hagenbeck's display of wild and trained animals which prefigured the modern zoo–the animals were housed in "a facsimile of the dens, lairs, mountain fastnesses and gorges which the wild animal loves to frequent." The demeaning exhibits of "native peoples" included nine Ainu, indigenous inhabitants of Northern Japan, who were brought over by way of Vancouver, complete with all their belongings and a dismantled house. Elsewhere, the Transvaal Military Spectacle featured the Boer War, fought twice a day for the amusement of visitors, with an extra matinee on Saturdays and holidays.

"Fair Japan"

Something of the changing American attitude to Japan in the years between Chicago and St. Louis is captured in these words written by a Japanese reporter in April, 1895:

> Ever since the Chicago Exposition foreigners have gradually acquired
> some knowledge of Japanese culture, but it has been limited to the
> fact that Japan produced beautiful pottery, tea and silk. Since the
> outbreak of the Sino-Japanese war last year, however, an attitude of
> respect for Japan may be felt everywhere and there is talk of nothing
> but Japan this and Japan that. Most amusing is the craze for Japanese
> women's costumes ...

The Sino-Japanese War had started several months after the Chicago Exposition. Japan initiated her next foreign military adventure, the Russo-Japanese War, nearly three months before the St. Louis Fair, with a surprise attack on the Russian fleet at Port Arthur. The conflict dragged on for more than eighteenth months, giving both sides a foretaste of the horrors of trench warfare and the deadliness of machine-gun fire. Japan was eventually victorious, thanks in no small part to its success in crushing the Russian fleet at the Battle of Tsushima in May 1905. Although Japan lost only 110 men at Tsushima, by the end of the war nearly 90,000 Japanese soldiers were dead and the economic and social costs were huge.

Against this background, the Japanese government went out of its way to ensure that the American public was favorably impressed by the industrial and artistic advances the emergent Asian super-power had made since 1893. According to an official Japanese report, there was at first some doubt as to whether Japan would take part at all as "she was busily engaged in preparing for the Fifth National Exhibition held in the city of Osaka in the last year [1903]," but when the inauguration was postponed until May 1904, Japan "was enabled to accept the invitation" and participate in a world's fair for the twenty-seventh time–a figure which must include some rather minor events. The report goes on to boast that although:

> ... there was only a short period of nine months until the opening of
> the Fair, and ... in the course of that comparatively short period the
> rupture of friendly relations between Russia and Japan greatly
> handicapped our endeavor concerning the Exposition, the officials
> in charge and the exhibitors worked in unison, pursuing their
> pre-conceived plan without a slight interruption ...

This was probably less than the whole truth, since the National Industrial Expositions were normally held in preparation for international shows, and other accounts suggest that representatives were sent to St. Louis a full year ahead of the opening. But in any event, the Japanese were the only foreign participants to complete their extensive displays ahead of time on April 18. Once again they secured a generous allocation of space in the main buildings, some 150,000 square feet in all, distributed between the Palaces of Industry, Manufactures, Education and Transportation, Mines, Agriculture, and Fine Arts. Overall, the display was twice as large twice as Chicago, and three times the size of the Japanese exhibits at Paris in 1900. The sum appropriated for Japan's official exhibits was $800,000, at that time equivalent to about 1.6 million yen–the total in 1893 had been 650,000 yen.

In addition to the exhibits in the Palaces, there were two other large Japanese outdoor areas at the Fair. One of these was the Imperial Japanese Garden, covering 15,000 square feet, where the original plans called for a replica of Nagoya Castle. In view of the imminent conflict with Russia, this was scaled down in favor of a replica of the Kinkaku [Golden Pavilion], an equally famous but smaller building in Kyoto built by a retired shogun at the end of the fourteenth century. A contemporary photograph shows the pavilion dwarfed by Ferris's giant observation wheel, which had been stored after the Chicago Fair and was erected a second time at St. Louis. The other major architectural reproduction was the Main Pavilion. This was a reduced version of the Shishinden, one of the buildings of the Imperial Palace in Kyoto, originally dating from the end of the eighth century, complete with the traditional cherry and *tachibana* [mandarin orange] tree standing at its entrance. There was also a Formosa Pavilion, representing the island of Taiwan, ceded to Japan after the Sino-Japanese War (1894–5), and the "Bellevue," a kind of exhibition of Japanese forest products, with no two pieces made from the same species of tree. In keeping with the twin-track cultural and commercial approach seen at both Philadelphia and Chicago, the dignity of the Palace and the Golden Pavilion was offset by an official bazaar which occupied a large section of the Imperial Garden next to the Commissioners' Office. Of all these official buildings the Kinkaku replica seems to have a struck the most sympathetic note with American visitors, partly perhaps because of its uncanny similarity to some of the traditional French-style buildings of the lower Mississippi region. A residence built in New Orleans in 1905 combines elements of the Kinkakuji with features of a Mississippi paddle-steamer, and the influence of the Japanese structure's multiple hipped roofs and deep eaves was seen as far afield as the Dreamland Air Ship Building at Coney Island. But it was the overall environment provided by the garden, rather than any particular building, which made the most immediate impression, as one commentator observed:

> The greatest attraction possessed by the village was in the grounds,
> which were so ornate with winding walks, bridges, fountains,
> pagodas, shrubbery and exotics that the garden seemed like a
> transplantation from Japan ...

The other outdoor Japanese area was the "Japanese Village" in the Pike, with at least two gateways, another bazaar called "Fair Japan," and a Japanese theater. The entrance was formed by a gaudy 100-foot-high replica of the Yomeimon Gate to the shogunal mausoleum at Nikko; a better quality version of this structure stood in the Palace of Varied Industries and was highly praised. There was also an original seventeenth-century two-storied temple gateway. This was later moved to Philadelphia and reassembled by Japanese workmen in Fairmount Park, on or near the site of the 1876 exhibition, where it survived until a fire in 1955. The Japanese entertainments in the Pike included one of the earliest performances in America of the popular traditional theater called *kabuki* (see Chapter two), the play on offer being the "Spider Play," a dramatic account of Raiko's struggle to overcome the monstrous "Earth Spider."

Developments in Japanese design

The Japanese section in the Palace of Fine Arts was in the West Pavilion next to the Bulgarian, Portuguese, and Italian displays, and covered 6,800 square feet compared to 2,850 at Chicago. The official record suggests that there were about 250 exhibits which a rigorous selection procedure had whittled down from the 713 originally submitted. The display eventually included 64 Japanese-style paintings, 28 Western- style paintings, 39 sculptures, and about 120 examples of decorative art including metalwork, lacquer, carving in ivory, bamboo and horn, ceramics, enamels, and textiles, as well as a small selection of designs for craft items and architecture. Before these works left Japan, 3,000 artists were invited by the government to visit the collection in Tokyo. The ceramic entrepreneur Yabu Meizan played a prominent part in the preparations. On August 15, 1903, he was appointed one of five Directors of the Louisiana Purchase Exposition Japan Exhibits Association, and he left Japan just eight days before the attack on Port Arthur, arriving at St. Louis on February 20. Meizan's adopted son Yabu Tsuneo worked as senior manager of the exhibit in the Palace of Fine Arts, and Meizan was permitted to show two pieces in this prestigious setting: a flower-shaped bowl with figures, now in the Walters Art Gallery (Baltimore) and another bowl with figures, birds, flowers, and landscape. Apart from brief mentions in the records of prize-winners and long lists of names, there is no detailed documentation of the wares displayed in other buildings of the Fair, but it is interesting that at this late date, even in the Fine Arts section, Meizan made little or no concession to the prevailing design trends discussed below. This did not, however, prevent him from both winning a gold medal in the Art Manufactures section and achieving his best-ever exhibition sales.

As well as Yabu Meizan's bowls, the illustrated catalogue of the Japanese exhibits in the Art Palace shows three vases by Kinkozan, the Kyoto "Satsuma" potter, that are in completely new style and techniques, with relief carving and the so-called *yohen* [transmutation] glazes also seen at an earlier date on the porcelain of Miyagawa Kozan. These changes were part of an evolution in the design of ceramics and some other decorative arts that had started in the mid-1890s and intensified in the light of critical comments made at the Paris Exposition of 1900. In 1901, the Nihon Zuan Kai [Japan Design Association] was established in order to stimulate the improvement of design, and a committee summed the problem up by noting that a few of the Paris exhibits–for example those by Kozan–had been highly praised, but they went on to say:

> However ... there are several areas demanding urgent improvement.
> These may be summarized in three points: firstly, the careful
> preparation of materials and the distribution of each kind of material;
> secondly, the improvement of the manufacturing process; thirdly,
> the shapes and designs.

These remarks concerned Japan ceramics, but the criticism of shapes and designs might equally have been applied to many of the other media on display in Paris. While Yabu Meizan seems to have ignored adverse criticism, for example the comments of Maeda Kasetsu which could have been made with him specifically in mind, a glance at the list of prize-winners at St. Louis makes it clear that the some of the most successful exhibitors had understood the need to rein in their decorative instincts and refine their shapes. Namikawa Sosuke in enamels, Miyagawa Kozan in porcelain, and Shirayama Shosai in lacquer–all represented in the Khalili Collection–won Grand Prizes for *Bijutsu seisaku genpin* [original art works], and their work certainly did move towards a greater simplicity and emphasis on form rather than surface decoration. This is particularly true in the case of enamels. Most of the technical improvements that occurred in the newly-discovered medium during the Meiji Era came about precisely because of the artists' determination to make their designs more open and more pictorial. At first, dense wirework was needed to hold the enamels on to the body during firing, but Namikawa Sosuke and his namesake Namikawa Yasuyuki succeeded in either reducing their dependence on wire or actually using it as an integral part of a pictorial design.

Another Grand Prize winner at St. Louis who had moved decisively towards pictorialism was Kawashima Jinbei II. Born into a family of Kyoto silk-weavers, he traveled to Europe in 1886, touring textile factories in France and Germany and admiring the tapestry-hung state rooms of the great royal and ducal palaces. Jinbei was especially impressed by France's Gobelins tapestry workshops and made a careful study of their manufacturing techniques, convinced that Japanese weavers, like their European counterparts, could create large-scale designs based on famous Old Master paintings, but with the difference that the originals would be Japanese rather than Western. The first fruits of his research, a series of tapestries in the Imperial Palace completed in 1888, were destroyed by bombing in 1945, but one of his earliest datable larger works–a completely new departure in the history of Japanese textiles–is a copy of a painting by Hara Zaisen, itself based on seventeenth-century depictions of the *inuoimono*, a kind of ritualized dog-hunt. Jinbei made an impressive contribution to the Chicago World's Fair, and his display at St. Louis was even more ambitious, consisting as it did of entire rooms hung with tapestries based on a famous series of paintings by the eighteenth-century painter Ito Jakuchu.

A lesson for Uncle Sam

By pressing ahead with design reform while maintaining or even improving the technical qualities of their wares, the leading Japanese exhibitors ensured that the critical reaction to the Japanese exhibits was generally favorable, if not as ecstatic as it had been at Chicago. But the recovery from Japan's failure at Paris was due to more than just aesthetic factors. The growing realization that Japan was likely to emerge triumphant from the Russo-Japanese War meant that the country's social and moral qualities came to be praised as much as its ingenious workmanship. Because China was officially exhibiting for the first time (at Chicago there had only been a private display in the Midway Pleasance), Japan also had an opportunity to show off her superiority to the Asian neighbor she had already humiliated in battle.

Like the Columbian World's Fair, the Louisiana Purchase Exhibition was celebrated in a number of multi-volume local publications such as J. W. Buel's ambitiously titled *Louisiana and the Fair: An Exposition of the World, Its People and Their Achievements*. Buel, whose semi-official middle-of-the-road opinions can probably be taken as a fair summary of informed reaction to the Japanese presence at St. Louis, commented that "in the manufacture of silk fabrics, satins, damasks, screens, fans, iron-ware and lacquered goods [the Japanese] are unapproachable" and "In the applied arts, in carvings, bronzes, pottery, decorative work, the Japanese are almost unequaled." Although this catalogue is confined to the decorative arts, it is worth noting that while Buel was quick to praise Japanese "deftness" he was much less flattering about efforts to emulate Western oil painting, noting that "… when they attempt canvases their lack of the reproductive talent, if one may use such an expression, is painfully apparent." In making this comment, Buel was reflecting a critical tradition going right back to Sir Rutherford Alcock, the British Minister responsible for the Japan display at the 1862 London International Exhibition, who had written, "Of high Art, such as has been cultivated in Europe since the dark ages, the Japanese know nothing." Buel may have been dismissive of efforts to emulate Western art, but his more general observations on the Japanese character show just how far Japan had risen in American estimation:

> … it is no exaggeration of their merits to say that in not a few respects
> Europeans may learn much from the Japanese. No people are more skillful,
> artistic, painstaking, reliable, truthful, loyal or courteous, and their sense of
> justice is likewise strongly marked. They have been called the Yankees of the
> east because of their ingenuity and indomitable courage, but they deserve
> also the designation of the Greeks of the east, for their military prowess and
> artistic instincts, which are not exceeded by any people of the world … Japan,
> small and poor, takes her place at the Exposition among the foremost powers
> of the world, while her gigantic adversary [Russia] has been deterred by the war
> from participating in any way in the Exposition except by individual exhibits.

Even in matters of design, it was no longer just the elaborate decoration of Japanese craft objects that was admired. Illustrations of contemporary American rooms suggest that exotic profusion was the keynote of most Japaneseque interiors before about 1900, but in 1904 "Samantha," a fictitious visitor to both Chicago and St. Louis, was delighted by the simplicity of Japanese domestic interiors, exclaiming:

> In cleanin' house time, now I have fairly begreched the ease and
> comfort of them Japanese housewives who jest take up their mat
> and sweep out, move their paper walls and little mebby and there
> it is done. No heavy, dirt-laden carpets to clean, no papered walls
> and ceilings to break their back over ... I set store by the Japans and
> am glad to hear how fast they're pressin' forwards in every path
> civilization has opened. They could give Uncle Sam a good many
> lessons if he wuz willin' to take 'em.

Sadly, no photographs seem to have survived of the simple rooms Samantha admired (they cannot have been the ornate interiors decorated by Kawashima Jinbei), but her comments suggest that they were precursors of the quite different image of Japanese design that has been so influential during the later twentieth century. For most of the Meiji Era, the Japanese had reacted skillfully to the prevailing American and European penchant for rich and inventive decoration, but by the time of the Paris Exposition their products were starting to lag behind developing international tastes. The gaudy archway on the Pike responded to a deep-seated popular vision of Japan, but many of the enamels, lacquers, and porcelains on display were moving in the direction of simplicity, even minimalism. While it would be several more decades before these qualities were perceived in the West as the essence of Japanese design, it can be argued that the emergence of a "less is more" aesthetic contributed to a more subtle view, not just of Japanese art, but of Japan in general. The fair included more than 80,000 Japanese exhibits of which only a tiny fraction were art objects of the kind illustrated on the following pages, and many serious visitors were probably just as impressed by such things as a full-size reconstruction of a mine or the first-class salon of a steamship. These achievements gave rise to concern that Japan had lost touch with her cultural roots, but the best works in the art display were perhaps admired precisely because they seemed to bring together elements of Japan's past, present, and future. Noting the progress shown by the Japanese in the decade since 1893, Walter Wellman wrote in *Success* magazine:

> At Chicago the Japanese appeared as interesting and picturesque makers of
> toys and knickknacks and articles of virtue of characteristic form but limited
> range–a sort of half-developed, peculiar people, with a hazy past not far
> removed from actual savagery and with an uncertain future. At St. Louis they
> appear as one of the first nations of the world.

THE JAPAN-BRITISH EXHIBITION

Although Japan took part in several other expositions in the early years of the twentieth century, the bilateral Japan-British Exhibition, held in London between May and October 1910, is perhaps the most interesting from the perspective of a collection of Meiji art that has been formed in the United Kingdom. The aim of the exhibition was to develop the diplomatic relationship with Japan that had been forged by the Anglo-Japanese Alliance of 1902. This was Japan's first formal alliance with a European power and it was in essence an imperialist pact, with the aim of thwarting Russia's plans for expansion in North-East Asia. In 1905 a second alliance was concluded that recognized Japan's claim to Korea and Britain's interests in India. During the Russo-Japanese War of 1904–5 there was widespread support in Britain both for Japan's war aims and for the courage of its fighting men, and the organizers of the 1910 exhibition built on the popular mood by including dioramas of recent Japanese military victories. Although the opening ceremonies had to be canceled because the court was in formal mourning for King Edward VII, the exhibition was a great success, attracting over eight million visitors–including a staggering 460,200 on September 24, Japanese Gala Day. The exhibition site at White City, named after the 1893 Chicago World's Fair, housed many of the features that had already become customary at international exhibitions, including a native Ainu village (an echo of 1904) and pavilions showing off the beneficial effects of Japanese colonial rule in Taiwan, Manchuria, and Korea, which was annexed by Japan in 1910 with little Western protest. The Japan-British

Exhibition contained a much wider range of art than had been seen in Britain before, including historical "treasures quite beyond price, the finest examples of their greatest masters of all periods, from the eighth to the nineteenth century." As well as copies and models of early architecture and lacquer objects belonging to the Imperial Household, there were "Japanese Women's Works, Education, Forestry, Arts and Crafts, Instruments ... and Applied Arts," shown in a wing of the Great Industrial and Machinery Halls. The displays were greeted favorably by visitors and critics, but some were disappointed by the lack of Eastern atmosphere, which was slightly offset by Japanese gardens laid out in the grounds of White City. As at St. Louis, a gateway formed an important part of the display, this time a four-fifths replica of the Chokushimon [Gateway of the Imperial Messenger] in Kyoto, commissioned by the Kyoto Exhibitors' Association. After the exhibition it was moved to London's Kew Gardens, where it has survived to the present day and was recently restored.

The Exhibition included over two hundred examples of contemporary Japanese art, mostly in the now-familiar categories: Japanese-style painting, Western-style painting, sculpture, ceramics, enamels, metalwork, dyeing and embroidery, and inlay, and the list of exhibitors reads like a role-call of some of the finest artists and factories: Kinkozan Sobei, Namikawa Sosuke, Ando Jubei, Kawade Shibataro, Unno Bisei, Kagawa Katsuhiro, Kajima Ikkoku, and Tsukada Shukyo. Because several of the pieces on view had also been shown at St. Louis, it is sometimes difficult to trace the development of design in certain categories, but the trends outlined above in connection with the 1904 selection had intensified, with even Yabu Meizan submitting a few pieces in the new style. The favorable critical reaction to these developments was aptly summed up in a comment on a vase by Miyagawa Kozan:

> ... a beautiful specimen of blue and white porcelain. It is a perfect
> piece both artistically and technically, very simple in line, and
> classic in shape, and quite artistic in the design of the matchless
> chrysanthemums, the pride of our country.

RUSSIA, JAPAN, AND THE UNITED STATES

Because the dates of this exhibition overlap with those of our previous show, *Nicholas and Alexandra: The Last Imperial Family of Tsarist Russia*, a few words are needed on interaction of these three nations during the last half of the nineteenth century. This brief overview may be regarded as an attempt to bring a sense of continuity to some of the public programs developed by Broughton International Inc. for these exhibitions.

Russian interest in Japan began with overtures extended during the reigns of Catherine the Great and her immediate successors, Paul I and Alexander I, in 1792 and again in 1804. All three monarchs wished to establish relationships with the Japanese, and all three attempts were rebuffed in succession. Nevertheless Russia did succeed in establishing fishing and hunting posts on the Kurile Islands. A series of petty raids then ensued, Russian attacking Japanese settlements on those islands in which it had established posts, and Japan retaliating by seizing an occasional Russian vessel, as occurred in 1811. Later, Tsar Nicholas I waged an unsuccessful campaign against Japan in 1852.

In time, Russian would redouble her efforts and those attempts would coincide with those of the United States, which was itself eager to gain a foothold in the Pacific Rim. In the aftermath of Commodore Perry's success, both Great Britain and Russia attempted to curry the favor of Japan inasmuch as both were at war with each other in the Crimea. The Russian admiral Putiatin, even after he lost his flagship in a tidal wave, was nevertheless so successful in his negotiations with the Japanese that his treaty with them gained Russia greater advantages than Perry's did for America. Moreover, Admiral Putiatin was able to include a clause in his treaty which divided the Kurile Islands between Russia and Japan. These goals were achieved in 1857. In 1875, Japan was able to reassert her claim to the northern Kurile Islands, but did so because Russian consent had been previously obtained in exchange for the Russian acquisition of Sakhalin.

During the period of the Meiji Restoration some members of the Iwakura Commission, charged with a formal government mission to visit Western government, opted to return to Japan via Russia at the mission's official conclusion in 1873, rather than via the Mediterranean, the route taken by some of their other colleagues. Relations between the two countries were such that a handful of Russian Orthodox priests were so successful at proselytizing Japanese that their Church could boast of 29,000 converts in 1907, an amazing number when one considers that there were only 60,000 Roman Catholics converts at the same time. Russia's stake in the Pacific Rim was clear and at odds with that of Japan, which was covetous of gaining control of over both Korea and Manchuria, the latter being a Russian objective as well. Russia did lay claim to Manchuria by taking possession of Port Arthur in Liaodong. This Russian expansion into Asia was due to an avaricious clique of greedy businessmen who aspired to enrich themselves from revenues gained in lumber. The construction of Russian-owned Chinese Eastern Railroad, begun earlier, which was to link Baikal and Vladivostock, was part of this picture. Russia had begun to ensnare Korea in an economic net in the form of a loan, the terms of which compelled Japan to deal directly with Russia to obtain prior confirmation of the archipelago's economic intentions with the peninsula. The defeat of China by Great Britain, coupled with French involvement in Indo-China, German in Shandong, and the Russian presence in Manchuria and influence in Korea were understandably disquieting to the Japanese.

Having toured the Orient during his youth and having visited Japan where he was attacked by a sword-welding assassin, Tsar Nicholas II considered himself an authority on things Oriental, so he took a very personal interest in developments with Japan. The economic interests of the lumber lobby enabled its members to flatter the tsar, and Kaiser Wilhelm of Germany, anxious to divert his cousin's attention for his own agenda in the Balkans, stroked the tsar's ego as well with such blandishments as "the Admiral of the Atlantic greets the Admiral of the Pacific." The Japanese did attempt to resolve the issue via compromise, but the lumber lobby convinced the tsar that it was not in Russia's best interest to accept the offer. War began between the two nations in 1904 when the Japanese attacked the Russian fleet at Port Arthur in Manchuria. Russian hopes for a speedy victory were universal as the propaganda machine of tsarist Russia rallied the nation against the Japanese people with the most racist of publicity campaigns. The sheer incompetence of the Russian high command, which led to humiliating losses, bred an ever increasing resistance against the war in the general public.

On January 22, 1905 the Tsar's troops fired on a group of peaceful demonstrators who had marched on the Winter Palace in St. Petersburg seeking an audience with the Tsar to review their grievances. Riots soon erupted nationwide and during the course of 1905 alone the nation's military was called out no fewer than 2,700 times to quell civil insurrection. In May of that year, the Russian fleet experienced its most humiliating defeat of the campaign at Tsushima. Its Baltic fleet had sailed half way around the world to engage in battle with the Japanese navy, only to be met and destroyed by the Japanese forces led by Admiral Togo Heihachiro. Russia could no longer sustain her war effort, and Japan recognized it could no longer maintain the economic expense demanded by the war and cope with the escalating number of its casualties. America stepped in with an offer to mediate, and brokered the peace at a conference held in Portsmouth, New Hampshire, presided over by President Theodore Roosevelt. The Portsmouth Treaty of September 5, 1905, acknowledged Japan as the dominant interest in Korea and mandated Russia's troop withdrawals from Manchuria.

The opening up of Japan by Commodore Perry may be regarded against the broader picture of America's political ideology of Manifest Destiny. According to this ideology America was fated, or bound, to occupy the great expanse of the North American continent which stretched from the Atlantic to the Pacific Ocean, all of the territories of which would be united under her sovereignty. California became part of the Union in 1848 at the expense of Mexico. That territorial expansion was to continue a decade after Perry's visit to Japan when then Secretary of State William H. Steward, serving under President Andrew Johnson, successfully negotiated the purchase of Alaska, an area of 591,004 miles, from Russia's Tsar Alexander II, the grandfather of Nicholas II, for the sum of

$7,200,000. Within this context, the continuing involvement of the United States in the affairs of the Pacific Rim in the later nineteenth century is more fully understood. Although immediate Japanese public reaction to the Treaty of Portsmouth was negative and led to rioting because Japan was not awarded an indemnity which the general public had been led to believe was its due, Japanese-Russian relations warmed. In the interval between 1907 and 1916, Tsarist Russia and Japan entered into a series of mutually beneficial agreements concerning their rights and interests in East Asia. All of the terms of these agreements were, however, subsequently unilaterally abrogated by the Bolsheviks as soon as they toppled the regime of Tsar Nicholas II. It is interesting to note that in the aftermath of the Russian Revolution, the Japanese became one of a handful of nations to intervene against the Bolsheviks. In 1918 it announced that it would be sending 12,000 soldiers to Siberia to assist the anti-revolutionary faction in Russia. Their number was eventually increased to 70,000 on the Japanese pretext that such a force was necessary to maintain Japan's national interest in Manchuria. This intervention was to be the cause for much of the hostility between the two nations for the remainder of the century.

THE AMERICAN WOMEN'S SUFFRAGE MOVEMENT

It may seem a bit strange at first to see a subheading in this Curriculum Guide dealing with the Meiji Era devoted to the American Women's Movement, but the unavoidable fact is that the influence of things Japanese on American society in part through the medium of the great international expositions intersected with the women's movement to produce some extraordinary crossovers. Many of these crossovers were due to the fact that the Japanese productions on view and for sale at the fairs were the catalyst for the emerging craft movement in America, a movement that was dominated by women.

The Philadelphia Centennial of 1876 witnessed the disruption of the opening ceremonies by the reading of the Declaration of Rights for Women, and one of the grandest of buildings there was the Woman's Pavilion. It is against this background that one can document the influence of "the Japanese craze" (as it was called at the time) on the women's movement. American women made things, many things for the home, which they arranged and decorated in an effort to reflect their taste. When one surveys the manifestations of this nineteenth-century American phenomenon, one finds that taste was dominated by Japan and things Japanese. This Japanese flavor even dominates what some would claim is the most American of America's home crafts of the period, the crazy or patchwork quilt. An editorial in *Art Amateur* of 1882 proclaimed:

> When the present favorite style of quilt was introduced it was called
> Japanese, but the national sense of humor has been too keen, and
> the Japanese is now generally known as the "crazy" quilt. There is
> method in its madness, however, and put together with a good
> understanding of color effects, the crazy quilt may prove an artistic
> piece of work. It its simplest form it is a combination of pieces of
> silk of every color and shape ... The materials are the waste scraps
> which collect in every house, too small or too irregular to serve
> any other possible purpose. These are reinforced by the exchanging
> of scraps between acquaintances ... One of the ambitions of a young
> man of fashion nowadays is the possession of a crazy quilt, made
> up of patches contributed by the ladies of his acquaintance; and his
> social progress may be reckoned by these patches as an Indian
> warrior's prowess is reckoned by his scalps.

The name was first applied to these quilts because the haphazard patterns of the scraps intersecting at various angles appeared to imitate the crackle of old china reproduced in the Japanese porcelains on view at the fairs. This influence, demonstrable as it is, is not of major concern here, but rather the effect that this Japanese craze had on American women in the arts. The American architect Henry Hudson Holly was able to suggest in 1878 that "There is, indeed, no reason why women should not become proficient, and be employed in all the industrial arts." That call was echoed by many individuals, among whom was Candice Wheeler, a woman whose life was of no particular interest until it took a turn after she visited a needlework pavilion at the Centennial. Immediately thereafter she was transformed into a leading advocate and role model for the career woman in the arts. With backing from a society matron, she formed the Society for Decorative Art of New York City which soon became the model for others in the Northeast. She went on to found the Women's Exchange which placed emphasis on marketing skills.

The involvement of American women in this craft movement was to have another, even more profound effect on American culture because it was these very women who formed organizations whose aims were to promote not only schools of art but also museums. For example, the Cincinnati Art Museum was founded in 1886 as the offspring of the Women's Centennial Executive Committee, the original mandate of which was "as an Association to advance women's work ... in the field of industrial art." Women were also instrumental in forming the contemporary Society of Decorative Arts in Hartford which gave new life to the Wadsworth Atheneum as well as the Rhode Island School of Design in Providence.

CHAPTER SIX

THE ARTS OF THE MEIJI ERA

The works of art on view in this exhibition represent some of the finest works of art–from both a technical and an aesthetic point of view–created during the Meiji Era in Japan from 1868–1912. Contemporary reaction to these pieces was uniformly lavish, whether the critic was European or American, and the impact of that art on the Occident was great. In the century or so between the end of the great international expositions and the present, the art of the Meiji Era has suffered somewhat of an eclipse, having been relegated to either a footnote or passed over altogether in silence in books about the history of Japanese art. Indicative of this lack of interest in things Meiji is the observation that as recently as the 1980s the level of connoisseurship and aesthetic appreciation of the art of the Meiji Era had reached such a nadir that there were virtually no scholars whose judgment could differentiate between a masterpiece and something that was run-of-the-mill. Dr. Khalili formed his collection not only to rehabilitate Meiji art in general, but also to restore its reputation to what it truly ought to be–an art which is unrivaled in its virtuosity and in the consummate mastery of the techniques used for its creation. As such this collection makes manifest Dr. Khalili's motto, formulated as his personal definition of this art: "Need, Art, and Craftsmanship are the three pillars of man's progress."

One of the salient characteristics of individuals is their inherent acquisitiveness–women and men seem born to collect. This desire to collect was keenly observed by the Meiji government, which recognized that patterns of collecting in the West which gravitated toward acquiring traditional Japanese art of the past, might equally be satisfied by promoting the acquisition of contemporary arts. If such new pattern of collecting could be developed, the thirst for Japanese antiquities might be somewhat slaked, and the drought of Japanese industry and increased productivity might be irrigated by the streams of Japanese craft productions pouring into Europe and America. It is important to remember that the fine distinction between arts and crafts, which some modern critics are at pains to maintain, did not always exist. In the late nineteenth century, for example, the philosophy which guided the programming at London's South Kensington Museum combined scientific technology with the arts. The Japanese government soon understood the efficacy of the marriage of arts with science and eventually established a separate division, the Hakubutsukyoku, or Exhibition Bureau, staffed initially by three competent individuals whose mandate was, among other things, to promote domestic and international participation in exhibitions at which art and science were joined. In keeping with this model, there was little regard for separating what one would term art from other manufactured, that is "made by hand," objects. Since the Japanese were attempting to preserve their ancient material cultures while promoting modern art, they formulated the philosophy of *koko rikon*, "study the ancient to benefit the present." Museum collections would house the ancient, the display and study of which would foster the production of high-quality contemporary works. As a result of these policies, works of art accounted for approximately 10 percent of Japan's exports during the period of the 1870s–90s.

METALWORK

In the transition period between the Edo Period and Meiji Restoration, of all of the traditional crafts none was so hard hit by the prospect of unemployment than metalwork. The shift away from Buddhism toward Shinto meant a decrease in commissions for ritual and temple implements crafted in bronze, and the dismantling of the samurai as an institution aborted the need for the continuing commissioning of the requisite weapons, primarily swords, and armaments in general. The change was even extended to mirrors which had traditionally been manufactured from polished bronze, but were now being replaced by the less expensive, mass-produced examples in glass and mercury.

Bronze-casters were soon able to fill the void by creating metal vases in either Chinese style, as they had done in the past, or by adapting their style to reflect new themes and motifs, which included the introduction of lions and elephants as a direct result of first- hand observation of these, and other beasts, at the recently opened Tokyo Zoo. Those who had lost income as a result of the *Haitorei*, or decree of 1876 banning the public wearing of swords, redirected their technical and aesthetic attention toward the manufacture of smoking sets, worn on the belt in place of the scabbarded sword, the principal element of which was the pipe. Others went on to create magnificent decorative objects such as the incense burners, free standing sculptures, and metal vases which are among the most spectacular metal objects on view in this exhibition.

ENAMELS

In Japanese cloisonné enameling, different areas of colored glass paste, separated from one another by thin strips of copper, gold, or silver ribbon (*cloisons*) placed edgeways and fixed to a copper base, are fired at about 1550–1650° F. until the paste melts and fuses. Although versions of cloisonné enameling have been known in the West for nearly two millennia and in China from about the four- teenth century, it made little headway in Japan until a few decades before the beginning of the Meiji Era when, according to tradition, a metal gilder called Kaji Tsunekichi (*b.* 1803) was inspired by the chance purchase of a Chinese cloisonné dish and decided to make a copy of it. There is no way of knowing whether the story of Kaji Tsunekichi is even partly true, but it does seem that the earliest Japanese cloisonné vessels surviving today, with dark-colored, rough enameling, were made in the 1850s, or perhaps a little earlier, in a crude imitation of Chinese prototypes.

After a slow start, Japanese enamelers were quick to exploit the new medium, winning a first prize at the Vienna Exhibition in 1873. A German chemist and polymath, Gottfried Wagener (1831–92), played a major role in the development of enameling in Japan. Wagener, one of many foreign experts who were invited to Japan to assist in the process of industrial and social reform, spent the last twenty-four years of his life there, advising craftsmen, building the first modern seismograph, and playing a crucial role in shaping Japan's contribution to the 1873 Vienna World Exhibition. Although the exact nature of his advice is not recorded, Wagener had previously worked as adviser on glazes and colors to the porcelain factories in Arita, and it is likely that he helped apply this exper- tise to the manufacture of enamels, including more sophisticated chemical compounds which–cru- cially for cloisonné–could withstand expansion and contraction during firing without leaving tell-tale cracks. This development helped put enamels in the forefront of design development during the later Meiji period, since it made it possible to break free of the mannered wirework of the Chinese tradi- tion and develop a new and essentially Japanese pictorial style. Wagener made a further contribution to this process by helping develop the so-called *shosen* [minimized wires] enameling in which the wires, generally very thin, are still visible but are used to delineate or emphasize part of the design as in a drawing, without necessarily forming a cell.

Wagener's advice was a critical factor in the careers of the two most famous enamelers of the Meiji Era, Namikawa Yasuyuki (1845–1927) of Kyoto and Namikawa Sosuke (1847–1910) of Tokyo. Despite their identically pronounced surnames (which are, however, written with quite different Chinese characters), the two men were unrelated, an odd fact which only served to heighten Western amazement at the seemingly miraculous output of their respective factories. Sosuke was always keen to promote his technical inventions, whereas Yasuyuki seems to have been altogether more conservative and retiring, though no less dedicated. His (or, more accurately, his employees', since both Yasuyuki and Sosuke were entrepreneurs rather than craftsmen) painstakingly precise method of working enables us to trace the development of his techniques and style with some accu- racy. The first tentative chronology for Yasuyuki's enamels was recently mapped out by the two editors of the Khalili Collection catalogues and their research has provided us with a framework for dating enamels by other leading workshops.

Recent discussion of Japanese enamels has tended to focus closely on technical changes and, in particular, on the technical difference between the works of the two Namikawas. It is worth remembering, however, that both of them were moving in much the same stylistic directions during the last decades of the Meiji Era. Both of them transcended the Chinese origins of their craft, improved it with European technology, and added the vital Japanese qualities of infinite patience and meticulous attention to detail. Their work, alongside that of Makuzu Kozan in porcelain, did much to fix a particular idea of "Japanese design" in the Western consciousness during the early years of the present century.

LACQUER

Japanese lacquer has been admired by the West since the sixteenth century when the first examples in that technique made their appearance in Europe, although the earliest Japanese lacquers date from the Jomon Period, about 4,000–3,000 B.C. Japanese lacquer is obtained from the sap of the lacquer tree, *Rhus verniciflua*, and its quality is dependent upon a number of variables from the quality of the soil in which the tree is growing, the time of year the sap is harvested, and the part of the tree from which the sap is obtained. Once harvested, the sap is refined in ways which again affect the quality of the finished product, as does the time of year at which it is applied in order for it to harden to optimum standards. Thanks to its unique physical and chemical properties, the viscous refined lacquer sap can be made to oxidize and polymerize so that it becomes hard, stable, and impervious, a process involving a chemical reaction between two constituents of lacquer, the ester urushiol and the enzyme laccase. This process will only take place if the temperature is between about 75–85 ° F. and the relative humidity is between about 80 and 85 percent. Japanese craftsmen developed a wooden cabinet, known as a *furo*, to control such factors artificially. As laborious as the preparation of the lacquer itself is the preparation of the object on which the lacquer is to be applied. The object must first be constructed to exacting standards and the lacquer must be applied in many separate layers, each of which must be allowed to set and then polished before the decoration of its uppermost layers can be effected. Quality lacquer provides a surface which is resistant to water, alcohol, heat, and mild acids, making it ideal of a variety of containers for the storage, preparation, and consumption of foodstuffs and beverages as well as for objects associated with writing–tables, document containers, and the like–and toilette objects such as combs, cosmetic boxes, and hairpins.

The most common method of decorating quality lacquerware during the Meiji Era was *maki-e*, literally, "sprinkled picture." The three types of *maki-e*, in order of historical appearance, are *togidashi-e*, *hiramaki-e*, and *takamaki-e*. In *hiramaki-e*, "flat *maki-e*," the simplest version of *maki-e*, the design is first drawn in ink on a thin, transparent piece of paper. The paper is then turned over and on its reverse the design is copied in outline only, using a very fine brush and thin lacquer which has been heated to remove its ability to set hard. The paper is laid, lacquer side down, on the surface to be decorated, and the design is transferred by rubbing it on the back. The design is then retraced with a fine brush in ordinary lacquer, which is often colored red. Before this lacquer has completely dried, the lacquered area is sprinkled with gold and silver powder from a tube made out of a piece of bamboo or the middle of a crane's feather. A fine gauze covering the end of the tube controls the flow of precious metal. This sprinkling process may sound simple enough, but it takes many years to master. Although dust that falls accidentally onto areas which have not been lacquered can easily be brushed away, within the lacquered area itself the density and exact distribution is determined entirely and irrevocably by the angle of the tube, its distance from the surface, and the amount it is shaken. After the lacquer has thoroughly set, another layer of lacquer is applied, and when this in turn has set, the design is polished. After further applications of lacquer and finer polishing, details can be drawn on the design, and these are subjected to the same process.

Two of the more elaborate versions of *maki-e* are *takamaki-e*, "high-sprinkled picture" and *togidashi-e* "polished-out picture." In *takamaki-e*, the design is built up in a mixture of lacquer with powdered clay or sawdust to get a three-dimensional effect. In *togidashi-e*, the completed *maki-e* design and its background are completely covered with several layers of lacquer. These are then gradually polished down until the original design starts to reappear, producing a brilliant flat polychrome effect. It is easy to describe these processes, but it should be emphasized that in order to become a skilled polisher, one needs to master the use of a range of different abrasives including stones, charcoal, pulverized horn, and cloth. Stones, in several grades of hardness, are used for the lower layers. Charcoal from, in ascending order of fineness and softness, magnolia, tung oil tree, crepe myrtle, and camellia, is used in combination with stones for the middle layers, and alone for the upper layers.

Japanese lacquered chests and cabinets probably first reached the West in the third quarter of the sixteenth century, a few years after the arrival of the first Portuguese sailors and about seventy-five years before Japanese porcelain (discussed below). The wares that were made for the new export market were quite different from those for Japanese buyers. Most were in European shapes, and the decoration was an exotic mixture of Japanese elements with motifs and patterns from China, Korea, and India, with lavish mother-of-pearl borders enclosing pictorial scenes or landscapes in gold lacquer. Japanese lacquered furniture made a striking addition to many European aristocratic and royal interiors during the seventeenth century, but it was never exported in anything like the same quantities as porcelain. Even though Japanese workshops introduced several new time-saving manufacturing methods, lacquerware, by its very nature, is not amenable to mass production. The trade reached a peak towards 1650, but from the 1680s the Japanese began to lose ground to cheaper Chinese imitations. Officially, the Dutch East India Company bought no lacquer after 1693, but as with porcelain, a small private trade continued until well into the nineteenth century.

Elsewhere in this catalogue we have seen how some Japanese crafts, particularly metalwork (above), struggled to survive the loss of their traditional markets and functions in the years around the Meiji Restoration of 1868. Although things were not easy for lacquerers in early Meiji, their situation was somewhat different, since some sectors of the industry were already in difficulties at the beginning of the nineteenth century, when *daimyo* families began to experience serious financial pressure as a result of a series of national economic crises. By the 1860s and 1870s, it is often said, *daimyo* families were selling off their treasured lacquer writing boxes and tables, or even scraping off and melting down the gold flakes. While it is impossible to know how much credence should be attached to these stories, it is clear that by the Meiji Restoration, several contradictory trends had emerged in the world of lacquer. In the domestic market, richly decorated classical wares were in decline but original, even eccentric work was being created for private buyers. Japanese lacquerers were also starting to make wares that responded to the Western taste for strange shapes and complicated designs. Since there was no tradition outside East Asia of working with true lacquer, lacquer craftsmen could not benefit from Western technological advances, as was the case in cloisonné enamels. To cope with rapidly increasing foreign demand, they had to devise ways of producing wares quickly and cheaply while maintaining high standards of workmanship. These two aims proved incompatible, with the result that although there are numerous examples of high-quality export lacquer work, many reveal an inevitable lowering of standards.

A new type of lacquerware called Shibayama, richly encrusted with coral, ivory, shell, and other materials, met part of the need for more rapid and easily appreciated effects. Other new types of lacquerware developed for the export market were distinguished from earlier pieces by unusual shapes and liberal use of striking techniques. In both Shibayama and more conventional lacquers, foreigners were also drawn to interesting subject matter, including views of famous tourist sites or episodes from ancient legends.

The dating of Meiji-Era lacquers is still a matter of controversy, but it is clear that from around 1890 onwards there was a revival of the classical style. This was connected with a general reawakening of interest in traditional artistic values that started in mid-Meiji and is symbolized, in the case of lacquer, by the appointment of Shirayama Shosai to the post of Professor of Lacquer at Tokyo Art School. Even in the 1870s, lacquerers and other craftsmen had been encouraged to make copies of historic lacquers, and in the 1880s a specialist company, the Onkosha, was set up to carry out such work in a more systematic way. Later works offer a foretaste of the new creative directions that Japanese lacquer would take in the twentieth century, when creative leadership, in lacquer as in other crafts, passed to graduates of Tokyo Art School and similar academic institutions elsewhere in Japan.

PORCELAIN

Unlike metalwork, pottery, enamels, and most types of lacquer, porcelain had been a major trade item between Asia and Europe since the late sixteenth century. The Chinese had, by that time, been making high-fired white-bodied ceramics for several hundred years, but in Japan, porcelain production did not start until about 1610–1620. The earliest porcelains were intended for the Japanese domestic market, but towards 1640 operations at the huge ceramic-producing center of Jingdezhen in central China were disrupted by civil war and economic dislocation. This meant that for a time the Chinese were unable to meet growing Western demand for porcelain, and from about 1650 until about 1740 very large quantities of porcelain were exported from Japan. The first major order, for over 50,000 pieces, was placed by the Dutch East India Company in 1659. Both the official trade and the private trade by the officers of the Dutch "factory" (trading post) at Nagasaki peaked in the 1680s, declining sharply after about 1740, although the private trade continued fitfully into the nineteenth century. The Japanese export porcelain phenomenon was a minor affair in comparison with its Chinese equivalent, but the very fact that Japan became known as a place which produced high-quality porcelain created the right conditions for a revival of the trade in the later nineteenth century.

This revival was due in large part to the efforts of one man, Miyagawa (or "Makuzu") Kozan (1842–1916), who took over his family's ceramic business in 1860 at the age of nineteen. During the 1860s Kozan made utensils for the Japanese tea ceremony (see Chapter two), but in 1871 he set up his kiln and shop in Yokohama and started to manufacture ceramics for the export market with the help of four apprentices from Kyoto. By 1877 he already employed at least eighteen potters and painters, including his adopted son and heir Miyagawa Hannosuke (Hanzan, 1859–1940).

During the 1880s, Kozan started to concentrate on producing the high-quality porcelain for which he is best known today, introducing a vast range of new decorative effects and techniques drawn both from Japanese and Chinese ceramic traditions and from newly developed Western techniques and styles. His success with flambé and crystalline glazes, widely admired both by collectors and by European factories attempting to reproduce the same effects, were officially recognized at the Paris International Exposition in 1889, where he won a gold medal.

Part of the secret of Kozan's commercial success lay in his ability to absorb not just new approaches to design, but also elements of Western ceramic technology. He frequently used imported chemical ingredients and his adopted son Hanzan acquired first-hand experience of Western techniques when he accompanied exhibits to the international fairs at Chicago in 1893, Paris in 1900, St Louis in 1904, and London in 1910. After the 1900 Paris Exposition, Kozan visited the Trent factories in England and the Rookwood Factory in America, and after the 1910 Japan-British Exhibition in London he made an extensive European tour.

In 1896 Kozan was awarded the position of *Teishitsu Gigeiin* [Artist to the Imperial Household]; he was only the second potter ever to receive this honor. He continued to exhibit successfully until his death in 1916, although it was always Hanzan who actually traveled to the foreign events, and at the time of the Japan-British Exhibition in 1910, Kozan would still be described in a magazine article as "the greatest living ceramic artist we have today in Japan." He was, in fact, more than that: one of the most remarkable figures of the Meiji Era, outstanding for his business acumen, his ability to respond to changing circumstances, his technical innovations, and his fidelity to Japanese artistic traditions.

An elaborately enameled and gilded ceramic ware called "Satsuma" captured the imagination of both European and American writers at the very start of the Meiji Era, and was perhaps the most extravagantly praised of all Japan's newly-discovered arts and crafts. In an early demonstration of Japanese skill in adapting product to market, it combined dazzling decoration with mysterious subject matter, both responding to prevailing Western taste and appearing to offer a privileged window onto the myths, legends, and customs of "old Japan."

The general term "Satsuma" could, if used correctly, cover all the pottery made in the Satsuma area at the southern tip of Kyushu, the southernmost of Japan's main islands. Kyushu has been a center of the ceramics industry since the 1590s, and Kyushu kilns had produced many different types of ware over the centuries, most of them looking nothing like Satsuma as we know it today. It was apparently not until the Paris 1867 Exposition that the term "Satsuma" was first used by Westerners to describe the gilded and enameled ware of the type featured in this exhibition. As a result of the ware's early success, orders began to come in from both Europe and America and very soon potters from other parts of Kyushu were helping to meet the demand.

Yabu Meizan of Osaka (1853–1934) was the most prolific of all the manufacturers of Satsuma ware. In 1880, after a time in Tokyo learning the art of pottery-painting, he opened the Yabu Meizan workshop in Osaka, buying his undecorated blanks from a kiln in Satsuma operated. During the economic depression of 1881–4, Yabu Meizan struggled to stay in business, but eventually he gained recognition and won a bronze medal at the Fourteenth Kyoto Exhibition in 1885. Throughout his career he continued to make full use of the marketing opportunities offered by both domestic and international expositions. His family still own many of the medals that he won at events from 1885 until 1916, in cities as diverse as Kyoto, Paris, Chicago, Hanoi, St Louis, Portland, London, Osaka, and Semarang in Dutch Indonesia. Most of his work is decorated in a minute style requiring extremely precise painting, which was achieved by using copper-plates for the designs. Looking at the best products of Yabu Meizan's workshop and of other craftsmen specializing in similar wares, we can readily understand just how it was that the combination of absorbing subject matter with infinitely painstaking craftsmanship exercised such a fascination among those Europeans and Americans who could afford the best work.

CHAPTER SEVEN

SPLENDORS OF MEIJI: THE EXHIBITION

GALLERY 1– EMERGENCE FROM ISOLATION

The Great Exhibition held at the Crystal Palace in London in 1851 inspired many similar events throughout the industrial world during the rest of the nineteenth century and the early years of the twentieth century. In an age before the development of long-distance mass media, these huge exhibitions or "world's fairs" gave leading nations and their colonies the opportunity to show off the best of their industry, culture, and society. As well as works of art like the pieces shown here, the largest expositions included halls devoted to such topics as agriculture, education, electricity, gardening, machinery, and even crime and punishment. Typically they took place in specially constructed buildings, included outdoor as well as indoor displays, and were enlivened by a host of extra attractions such as "native villages," bazaars and fairgrounds. The numbers attending them were huge and they often covered vast areas.

Japan quickly realized the importance of the world's fairs, and had participated in two of them in the period immediately preceding the Meiji Era, but the Meiji government's first formal involvement in a world exhibition took place at the Vienna World Exhibition in 1873, to which the Japanese committed no less than 0.8 percent of their gross national product. Japan's success at this and later events was the result of centralized organization, meticulous preparation, and early recognition of the need to cater to Western interests. In order to compensate for Japan's dearth of modern industrial products, the new Japanese government focused its attention on showcasing traditional art and crafts, which, in the period between the 1870s and 1890s, accounted for nearly 10 percent of her exports. This exhibition is about that art. It was created from about 1870 to 1910, and flourished as a direct result of government sponsorship and the occasional patronage of the emperor and his family. This official support created an ideal environment in which leading craftspeople were able to refine the skills they had inherited from their Edo-Period forbears. Bronze-casters, for example, who had earlier produced bells, gongs, and statuary for the Buddhist religion, were forced to redirect their efforts to new creations such as the large decorative incense burners and vase on view in Gallery 1. Reapplying those techniques made it possible for them to produce works of a technical excellence not seen before or since. They were joined in their efforts by other specialists working in porcelain, enamel, lacquer, and other traditional media. Government sponsorship insured the highest standards, and the Japanese displays at the international exhibitions were always among the most highly praised.

GALLERY 2–THE BEAUTY OF JAPAN IN AMERICA: PHILADELPHIA 1876

Although Philadelphia's Centennial Exhibition of 1876, scheduled to coincide with the hundredth anniversary of the founding of the United States of America, was first proposed in 1866, actual planning did not begin March 1871, when Congress passed an act establishing the United States Centennial Commission. A Centennial Board of Finance was created the following year in order to manage the budget, and in 1874 officials were appointed so that construction might begin on a site in Fairmount Park by the Schuylkill River. The exhibition was large, covering 236 acres.

The Japanese first learned about the American centennial celebration in June 1873 but did not decide to participate until the following year. That decision was accompanied with a commitment of the equivalent of $600,000 to the event, an amount which represented the largest sum invested by any of the thirty participating nations. The Japanese created a Centennial Office, placed under the control of the newly formed Board of Commerce, Trade, and Agriculture, which enlisted a corps of foreign advisors, and sent a representative to Philadelphia to head up a local office aimed at ensuring that Japan's three objectives were met, namely freedom to arrange their material according to their own dictates, a greater amount of space than initially offered, and the ability to sell that material at the fair's conclusion.

In a pattern repeated at many international arts events down to the present, the Japanese even erected a Japanese dwelling for their high officials, built by Japanese workmen sent specifically to Philadelphia for that purpose. They also created the very first Japanese garden in America. The workmen's activity, uniforms, and comportment excited widespread comment and a great deal of pre-opening publicity.

On Opening Day, May 10, the size and splendor of the Japanese exhibition made a deep and favorable impression on visitors and press alike. The display, overhung with large Japanese flags and long banners decorated with the imperial chrysanthemum crest, was arranged on two diagonal platforms with a one-hundred-foot frontage. The entrance was flanked by two elaborate five-foot high bronzes. In fact, bronzes were a prominent feature of this exposition and were described by one commentator as "the most marvelous objects here." Visitors mentioned in particular a bronze vase surmounted by an eagle with flights of birds forming its handles, as well as bronze cranes, tortoises, hens, and rabbits. One of the centerpieces was a formidable display of ceramics arranged on a wedding-cake-like stand twelve feet high, with examples from many of the main Japanese kilns, ranging in size from huge Arita porcelain vases to tiny tea cups. Other cases were filled to the brim with lacquer, ivory, and more metalwork.

The ten million visitors to Philadelphia in 1876 were deeply impressed by the novelty of the Japanese displays and fascinated by the contrast between Japanese design and the predominantly High Victorian style of the works of art on view in the European pavilions. The appeal of Japan to her American audience may also be attributed, on one level, to the same reason that had made Commodore Perry the right man to open up that country twenty-three years earlier. Namely, both nations were new to the international scene and felt that they could deal with each other on equal terms. Yet, on another level, Americans as children of the Industrial Revolution shared with Europeans their admiration of Japan's antiquity, real or imagined, as it was presented in the objects at this fair. They imagined Japanese craftsmen, laboring with their hands, existing in an environment freed from the shackles of the machine and the concomitant ravages of the Industrial Revolution. The Japanese government capitalized on such sentiment, as revealed by the following statement in the official Japanese government guide to the Philadelphia Centennial Exhibition which claimed that "the Japanese artisan is still very much like those of medieval Europe working in his own peculiar way, assisted only by a very few assistants, and being himself both artist and artisan." Statements like this made Japanese art all the more popular as people in the West became increasingly concerned about the dehumanizing effects of industrialized mass production in their own countries.

GALLERY 3–JAPAN WELCOMES THE WORLD: THE NEW MARKETPLACE

After the Treaty of Kanagawa was signed by Japan and the United States in 1854, America and the major European nations pushed ahead with demands for trading privileges and the right to "extraterritoriality," meaning that foreign nationals could live in designated areas subject to the laws of their own countries rather than those of Japan. In 1858 Townsend Harris, the first U.S. Consul-General, submitted a Treaty of Amity and Commerce under which a further six ports would be opened to foreign trade. One of these was to have been Kanagawa, a town in the south of Tokyo Bay on the main road between Tokyo and Kyoto, but the Japanese decided it would be better to confine the foreigners to the more secluded fishing village of Yokohama, a few miles away. Little did the Japanese imagine the future success of this village.

A decisive factor in Yokohama's development was the new railroad connecting the port with the capital city, Tokyo. When the line was eventually opened in 1872 the ceremony was performed by the emperor himself, attired in the cumbersome traditional court dress. Soon the Bay of Yokohama was filled by ships of many different nations, providing an appearance, in the words of one visitor, not unlike that of a port of some American town with verdant hills, and, weather permitting, a glimpse of the distant sight of Mount Fuji. By 1893, the year in which worldwide steamship tonnage overtook sailing-ship tonnage for the first time, Yokohama was a nexus of global communications and tourism.

The 1880s witnessed the emergence of a world-wide craze for Japanese artistic goods of all kinds, and Yokohama rapidly became the natural, if not the preeminent Japanese center for the production and sale of the finest work that Japan's resurgent craft industries, already boosted by government sponsorship and trade initiatives, had to offer. Yokohama's status as the focus of a "Japanese Craze" that was then sweeping the Western world also made it a magnet for unscrupulous dealers who were only too eager to peddle inferior wares to the less well-informed tourists, often passing them off as items of great antiquity. Discriminating critics were, nevertheless, able to distinguish between "run-of-the-mill" productions and those of the high aesthetic value seen in the pieces displayed in this gallery.

GALLERY 4 – AN ISLAND EMPIRE OF MYTH AND MYSTERY

Throughout the Meiji Era, American and European connoisseurs were fascinated by the exotic stories depicted in the elaborate decoration of Japan's treasured bronze, lacquer and ceramic works of art. Their imaginations were fired as well by a series of Western authors and composers whose combined output did much to keep things Japanese on the public's mind. Many of these visions of Japan are themes derived from her religions. Shinto, literally meaning "the way of the *kami*," is a belief system native to the Japanese archipelago in which whatever seemed strikingly impressive, possessed of a quality of excellence, or inspired a feeling of awe, was called *kami*. The word *kami*, therefore, encompasses a polytheistic host, whose members, like those of other very ancient animistic belief systems, inhabit nature on every level so that in principle human beings, birds, animals, trees, plants, and even mountains and the ocean may all be *kami*.

Buddhism, on the other hand, developed in the North India from the teachings of Gautama (about 563–483 B.C.), the historical Buddha. The fundamental principle of Gautama's doctrine regarded the world as a place of universal suffering brought about by twin, basic human impulses, namely desire and acquisitiveness. Enlightenment, or a release from this state of worldly suffering, could be achieved by adherence to an eightfold program. As influential as the teaching of Gautama were, his principles were modified about a half a millennium after his death by the development of Mahayana, a system with a bewilderingly complex pantheon of different Buddhas and exalted beings.

Shinto and Buddhism have since become a feature of the religious landscape of Japan, and have usually flourished in a state of peaceful coexistence or even interdependence. Upon assuming power in 1868, however, the Meiji government took rapid steps to downgrade Buddhism in favor of Shinto, the native religion, which was seen to embody the authentic values and historic destiny of the Japanese people. Another important ethical system in Japan is Confucianism, the Chinese corpus of moral and political philosophy that was first expounded by Kong Fuzi (a name that was later Latinized to Confucius by Jesuit missionaries) in the fifth century B.C. Although known in Japan since the fifth century A.D., Confucianism was not widely disseminated among the Japanese elite until the seventeenth century. Confucianism emphasizes the importance of harmonious social relationships and loyalty to righteous rulers as well as to fathers, husband and elder brothers. As such, it was a valuable ideological tool and was used both by the shoguns and, after a brief interlude, by the Meiji government to underpin their authority.

Equally important as a source for themes employed to decorate the art of the Meiji Era was the geography and topography of Japan. The first intrepid Western explorers were able to take advantage of a network of roads and simple wayside inns that led them, often in great discomfort, to such established beauty-spots as the great mausoleum at Nikko in the mountains north of Tokyo, the bridge at Uji, the architectural splendors of Kyoto (the former capital and the cultural center of the country), and of course the volcanic cone of Mount Fuji, the "peerless mountain." Visitors to the exhibition *Splendors of Meiji* may at first be somewhat perplexed by the profusion of decidedly Chinese subjects depicted on the art the period. In this choice, the craftsmen were following the lead of their predecessors of the Edo Period. Particularly popular are motifs drawn from a vast vocabulary of subject matter based on the Chinese Ming Dynasty (1368–1644), as well as themes related to Confucianism, which was revived in the mid-Meiji Era for political reasons because of its emphasis on loyalty and obedience, as well as the need for kings and emperors to rule virtuously. Chinese mythical creatures, especially the dragon, a symbol of imperial power, continued to be a favorite subject, particularly on porcelain.

No Japanese institution seems to have captured the imagination of the West more emphatically than that of the samurai, literally meaning "one who serves." The word describes a class of warriors, each owing unswerving allegiance to his feudal lord, who first came to prominence in Japan's civil wars of the twelfth century. European and American writers contemporary with the Meiji Era quickly came under the influence of the mystique of this traditional warrior class. The period's popular literature, drama and art often depicted the samurai as heroic figures whose conduct was guided by a selfless moral code. This image of the samurai coincided with renewed Western interest in the chivalric ideals of Europe's medieval knights, and they became a favorite subject for the decoration of items intended for export to Europe and America.

GALLERY 5–THE GOLDEN AGE OF MEIJI: CHICAGO 1893

Americans, aware of the approach of the four-hundredth anniversary of Columbus's discovery of America, resolved to celebrate the event with a spectacular. It was ultimately decided that the festivities would be best served by staging another great international world's fair, and Chicago was selected as the site. By 1890, however, it became apparent that preparations could not be completed in time, with the result that the World's Columbian Exposition opened on May Day 1893, although a formal dedication ceremony was conducted on the site late in 1892 to demonstrate that the fair actually began in the year of the anniversary. The Chicago fair proved to be the greatest of the nineteenth century's international expositions. It covered a total of 688 acres in Jackson Park along Lake Michigan, and attracted 27,539,000 visitors, a number equal to almost one quarter of the then population of the United States. There was even a giant wheel 250 feet in diameter built by a Mr G. W. G. Ferris of Pittsburg which could carry 2,160 people at a time in 36 cars. One of the more exotic sights of the fair was erected on the Wooded Island, located in a lagoon near the United States Government Building. Here the Japanese constructed the Ho-oden [Phoenix Palace], an adaptation of the eleventh-century Ho-odo [Phoenix Hall] at Uji, a town to the south of Kyoto. It was the seventh largest national building on the fair grounds, landscaped and planted in Japanese style.

Japan, the only Asian nation granted a place in the prestigious setting of the Palace of Fine Arts, even managed to get the amount of space allotted to it there doubled in the course of the fair. Care was taken to ensure that the objects selected for this honor were of the very highest quality, and could be easily distinguished from the more commercial wares on view elsewhere. To that end, the Japanese commissioners persuaded the American organizers to allow them to display their objects in three separate areas in a method which was contrary to the way in which America and the European nations were displaying their art. By doing so, the Japanese were able to play down their painting and sculpture, which they knew would not make such a favorable impression on the public, in order to showcase their spectacular works of porcelain, cloisonné enamel, textiles, and metalwork.

The selection of Japanese art and its presentation in Chicago succeeded in creating an overwhelmingly favorable impression. Admiration for things Japanese continue to grow, and was to have a very profound effect on some of the most unexpected quarters of American culture, particularly on architecture. One of the foremost architects of the day was Louis Sullivan, who in collaboration with Frank Lloyd Wright, was actually responsible for the designs of a few of the buildings at the fair. In the year in which the fair opened, Wright elected to sever his association with Sullivan and start his own office. His "organic architecture," in which form followed function, was greatly indebted to the Japanese for its inspiration. Throughout his long career Wright continued to admire Japanese design and craftsmanship, in particular for the way it respected the inherent qualities of the materials used.

GALLERY 6–A NEW CENTURY: ST LOUIS 1904

St. Louis lost its bid to host the 1893 World's Fair but prevailed as the next American venue for an international fair when it hosted the Louisiana Purchase Exposition in 1904. It was even bigger in size and scope than the Chicago event, although it drew approximately eight million fewer visitors. The entire site was constructed in less than three years despite 200 labor disputes. The fair grounds, which included more than 1,500 buildings spread over 1,272 acres, opened to the public on May Day 1904. Nearly three months before that date Japan had embarked on a war against Russia, making a surprise attack on the Russian fleet at Port Arthur in Manchuria and landing its troops in Korea. In spite of this difficult situation, the Japanese government once again went out of its way to ensure that visitors to a great American fair were favorably impressed by the emergent Asian superpower. In addition to the places occupied by their objects in the various buildings at the Fair, the Japanese created four additional attractions. The first was the Imperial Japanese Garden, covering 15,000 square feet, which featured a copy of the Kinkaku, or Golden Pavilion at Kyoto. Visitors were so taken by the garden because its effect with its winding walks, footbridges, fountains, pagodas, shrubbery, and exotics seemed to have been literally transplanted from Japan.

The Lousiana Purchase Exposition also included an amusement area, called the "Pike," which was much better remembered than other aspects of the fair itself. The entrance to the "Japanese Village" in the Pike was formed by a gaudy 100 foot high replica of the Yomeimon Gate to the shogunal mausoleum at Nikko. Other appointments of the Japanese Village included an original seventeenth-century two-storied temple gateway, which was later moved to Philadelphia and reassembled by Japanese workmen in Fairmount Park, on or near the site of the 1876 exhibition. This gateway survived until 1955, when it was destroyed by a fire. Within the Japanese Village a visitor could also find another bazaar called "Fair Japan," and a Japanese theater. Here was staged one of the earliest performances in America of the popular traditional theater called *kabuki*. The performance was that of the "Spider Play", a dramatic account of Raiko's struggle to overcome the monstrous "Earth Spider."

The Japanese section in the Palace of Fine Arts was in the West Pavilion next to the Bulgarian, Portuguese, and Italian displays. Selection of the objects for display here was rigorous. Official records reveal that only about 250 works of Japanese art, out of a total of 713 submitted, were judged to meet the criteria established. Some of the works exhibited differed from those shown at early world's fairs. These artistic and technological changes were part of an evolution in the design of both ceramics and other decorative arts that had started in the mid-1890s and intensified in the light of critical comments which Japanese officials were still collecting and studying in order to stimulate the improvement of design. In general, therefore, there was a perceptible movement in Japanese art at the time towards a greater simplicity and emphasis on form rather than surface decoration. This was particularly true in the case of enamels. Most of the Meiji Era's technical improvements in that newly-discovered medium were the direct result of the artists' need to create designs which were more open and more pictorial. Americans appointed the rooms of their homes in accordance with their perceptions of Japanese design tenets. Even a brief glance at the many surviving photographs of the interiors of American homes and college dormitories of the period before 1900 suggests that exotic profusion was the keynote of most of these Japaneseque interiors, a profusion encountered as well in the decoration of contemporary Japanese export production which relied upon elaborate decoration for its effect. That aesthetic changed, as the prevailing Japanese idiom at St. Louis reveals, in favor of simplified designs and refined shapes of vessels. This shift was admirably conveyed in a description written in 1904 by Samantha, a fictitious visitor to St Louis, who was delighted by the simplicity of Japanese domestic interiors, and quaintly explained how the Japanese housewife, in such an environment, could with less time and energy maintain a spotless home in contrast to her American counterpart who had to contend with thick carpets and floor to ceiling wall paper.

GALLERY 7– ARTISTS TO THE IMPERIAL HOUSEHOLD

In keeping with other aspects of human endeavor in the Meiji Era, artistic policy was decided by bureaucrats who commissioned reports and studies examining the criteria by which foreign judges had awarded prizes at the internationals, and scrutinized their every comment in what turned out to be a highly effective method of determining future market trends. These same bureaucrats organized government-sponsored institutions in an effort to promote Japanese art at those fairs. The system known as *Teishitsu Gigeiin*, "Artist to the Imperial Household," was the logical extension of the prevailing official policy that had been in place almost from the start of the Meiji Era. Governmental commissions ensured that the best artists and entrepreneurs could, when the occasion demanded, lavish the time and energy on the media at their disposal in order to create works of art meeting the highest standards of the day. As an extension of this kind of governmental support, it was suggested in 1880 that long-term preferential treatment should be extended to selected artists under the patronage of the Imperial Household. And so it was that in April 1888 the statesman and art administrator Sano Jomin took formal steps to put this idea into practice by making an appeal to the Imperial Household Minister. His initiative eventually resulted in a meeting held in February 1890 during which the first individuals honored with the title *Teishitsu Gigeiin* were appointed. It must be remembered that the *Teishitsu Gigeiin* system was in effect a governmental body which simply operated in name of the emperor. To the best of one's information, few of that governmental body's decisions seem to have been influenced by the emperor's personal tastes or aesthetic judgments.

The earliest recipients of the title were painters and sculptors rather than lacquerers, potters, metalworkers, and enamelers. Although the stated aim of the program was to promote Japanese art, preserve old techniques, and encourage future generations, one gains the distinct impression that the criteria employed for the selection of honorees included within the first list placed great value on distinguished elderly citizens for a lifetime's contribution to cultural life. Seven of the eleven so initially honored would be dead by the end of the century. Of seventy individuals appointed to the order of *Teishitsu Gigeiin* between 1890 and 1944, twenty-four were lacquerers, potters, metalworkers, enamelers and swordsmiths, and their proportion in relation to those in other media remained higher in the early years down to 1906. The porcelain artist Seifu Yohei, always better appreciated in Japan than overseas, was appointed in 1893. The year 1896 witnessed the appointment of the largest ever number of decorative artists. These included Unno Shomin and Suzuki Chokichi in metalwork, Namikawa Yasuyuki and Namikawa Sosuke in enamels, Miyagawa Kozan in porcelain, Kawanobe Itcho and Ikeda Taishin in lacquer, and Kawashima Jinbei in textiles. Shirayama Shosai was eventually appointed in 1906, perhaps in recognition of the success his lacquers achieved at St. Louis, as was the metalworker Kagawa Katsuhiro. The three remaining *Teishitsu Gigeiin* included in this exhibition would not be appointed until after the death of the Meiji emperor: Tsukada Shukyo in 1913 and the potters Ito Tozan and Suwa Sozan in 1917.

Upon appointment, *Teishitsu Gigeiin* had to submit one example of their work. They were also expected to accept commissions from the Kunaisho, or the Imperial Household Department, and to prepare reports for the Imperial Museum. In return, they received an annual stipend of 100 yen. Some of the commissions were for presentation wares, and these, particularly the vases, bear the imperial sixteen-petaled chrysanthemum and are often of a standardized shape and uniform height of approximately 18 inches. The Imperial Household Department seems to have had a policy of stockpiling presentation wares for future use: the most ambitious imperial gift in the Khalili Collection, a lacquer cabinet presented by the Crown Prince Hirohito to the British Prince of Wales in 1921, was apparently kept in storage in Japan for ten years. In 1912 all of the *Teishitsu Gigeiin* were engaged, each in their own metier, on a work to be presented to the Emperor Meiji on the occasion of his sixty-first birthday as a token of the nation's appreciation for his encouragement of the arts. The presentation was scheduled to take place on November 3, 1912, but had to be canceled because of the emperor's untimely death. The presentation pieces were completed and subsequently presented in the emperor's memory to his successor. They eventually found their way into the Imperial Household Museum. The pieces in this gallery similarly date from late in the careers of their makers, in most cases after their appointment as *Teishitsu Gigeiin*. Among the finest works in the whole of the Khalili Collection, they form a fitting tribute to an era in which imperial patronage and government sponsorship enabled such masterpieces to be created.

(1641) Following a period of persecution of Christianity, the shoguns' policy of seclusion is completed with the move of the Dutch trading post to the small island of Deshima in Nagasaki Harbor.

(About 1620–1700) Exported Japanese lacquer and porcelain are popular in Europe for a time, until Chinese products begin to dominate the Western market in the late 1600s.

(1716–ca.1800) Controls on foreign goods are relaxed and limited quantities of Western (particularly Dutch) books and scientific instruments begin to be imported. A few Japanese start to take an interest in so-called "Dutch studies" and some of them begin to warn of the need to protect Japan against foreign invasion.

(About 1800–68) Sporadic Japanese contact with Western countries, and the westward expansion of the United States, culminate in Commodore Perry's 1854 mission. Under pressure from the United States and other Western powers, Japan signs trade agreements and allows limited access to foreign trade and diplomacy. There is a growing conflict within Japan about the best way to counter the foreign threat, but eventually a group of reforming samurai deposes the shogun and establishes a new government. Japanese craft goods are exhibited in Europe for the first time.

(About 1800–41) Growth of the North Pacific whaling industry leads to occasional contacts between Western ships and survivors from Japanese wrecks. In 1837, the *U.S.S. Morrison* unsuccessfully tries to land Japanese castaways near Edo, and in 1841 a young Japanese whaler, John Manjiro, is rescued up by an American ship, eventually reaching New Bedford, Massachusetts and not returning to Japan until 1851.

(1842) Great Britain's easy victory over China in the First Opium War alerts Japan to the dangers of encroachment by the Western powers.

(1846) Commodore James Biddle leads the first, unsuccessful U.S. diplomatic mission to Japan; a second mission in 1849 under Commander James Glynn is also unsuccessful.

(1848) California achieves independence from Mexico and enters the Union.

(1849) The California Gold Rush.

(1853) Commodore Matthew C. Perry visits Japan with the largest United States fleet ever seen in the Pacific and demands that Japan establishes trading and diplomatic relations.

(1854) Commodore Perry "opens" Japan. Japan and the United States sign a Treaty of Peace and Amity, known as the Treaty of Kanagawa, on March 31. Japanese objects are exhibited in London for the first time.

(1856) Townsend Harris (1804–78) arrives in Japan as the first United States Consul-General.

(1858) The United States and Japan sign a Treaty of Amity and Commerce, known as the Harris Treaty, despite court disapproval. Japan signs similar "unequal" treaties with Great Britain, France, Russia, and the Netherlands.

(1859) Yokohama is officially opened to foreign residents.

(1860) Ii Naosuke, a leading advocate of treaties with foreign powers, is assassinated by an anti-foreign fanatic. Similar assassinations now follow throughout the rest of the country. The Tokugawa shogunate sends its first mission to the United States.

(1861) The Takenouchi diplomatic mission is sent to Europe.

(1862) The British Minister Sir Rutherford Alcock organizes a Japanese display at the Second International Exhibition in London.

(1866) Japan signs tariff agreements with the United States, Great Britain, France, and the Netherlands.

(1867–68) Civil war rages in Japan. The forces of the Satsuma, Choshu, Hizen, and Tosa domains are victorious over the forces of the Tokugawa shoguns.

(1867) The shogunate participates in the Paris Universal Exposition at the invitation of the French government, sending more than 1,300 objects. The Emperor Komei dies in January. The last shogun, Tokugawa Keiki, tenders his resignation on October 14.

(1868–77) The new government of Japan consolidates it power, introduces basic reforms, and promotes the export of raw silk, tea, and craft goods.

(1868) The Meiji, "Enlightened Government," Restoration reestablishes imperial power in the person of the fifteen-year-old Meiji emperor. The emperor moves to the new capital, Tokyo. An edict separates Buddhism and Shinto.

(1870) Shinto is declared the national religion.

(1871–73) The Iwakura Mission travels to the United States and Europe to study Western institutions and technology.

(1871) All the provinces and feudal domains are replaced by prefectures and the tax system is centralized.

(1872) A steam railroad between Shinagawa (Tokyo) and Yokohama is formally opened by the Meiji Emperor. The first government-sponsored exhibition is held in a Tokyo temple. Universal compulsory primary education is introduced.

(1873) Japan plays a major part in the Vienna World Exhibition, devoting nearly one percent of the national expenditure to the event. Military conscription for men is introduced.

(1874) The Kiritsu Kosho Kaisha Trading Company is set up after the Vienna Exhibition to promote Japanese crafts in the United States and Europe.

(1876) Japan plays a major part in the Philadelphia Centennial Exhibition. The Kiritsu Kosho Kaisha opens a branch in New York at 865 Broadway. The samurais' annual salaries are ended and they are forbidden to wear swords in public.

(1877) The first Domestic Industrial Exposition is held in Tokyo. A rebellion led by the conservative Saigo Takamori is put down by government forces.

(1877–89) Its power secure, the new government presses ahead with a program of industrialization and political, legal, social, economic, educational, and military reforms. A more critical attitude develops towards the West and Western art.

(1878) Paris Universal Exposition.

(1879) The Ryuchikai Society is formed to reawaken Japanese interest in Japanese art forms and resist excessive Westernization. General Ulysses S. Grant visits Japan.

(1881) The second Domestic Industrial Exposition is held in Tokyo. Plans begin for the creation of a National Diet, or Congress.

(1884) The Rokumeikan Building opens and becomes a symbol of wholesale Westernization.

(1885) Japanese works are widely acclaimed at the Nuremburg International Metalwork Exhibition.

(1889–1912) Japan establishes itself as a world power, ending the system of "unequal treaties" with the West, winning two international wars, and embarking on a period of strong economic growth dominated by powerful industrial conglomerates.

(1889) Paris Universal Exposition. The Tokyo Art School opens. The Meiji Constitution is promulgated, declaring the divinity of the Emperor and establishing a two-chamber parliamentary system, but giving most of the real power to the cabinet.

(1890) The Imperial Museum (later the National Museum) opens. The third Domestic Industrial Exposition is held in Tokyo. The first Craftsmen to the Imperial Household are appointed. The first Diet convenes.

(1891) The Kiritsu Kosho Kaisha Trading Company is closed. A nationalist fanatic attempts to assassinate the Tsarevich, later Russian Tsar Nicholas II, at the beginning of a state visit to Japan. This incident was recalled in our previous exhibition, *Nicholas and Alexandra. The Last Imperial Family of Tsarist Russia.*

(1893) The Japanese exhibits at the Columbia World's Fair in Chicago attract widespread acclaim.

(1894–95) Japan's victory in the Sino-Japanese War symbolizes its rapid modernization and extends its control over Korea.

(1895) The fourth Domestic Industrial Exposition is held in Kyoto.

(1899) A treaty with Great Britain ends the practice of "extraterritoriality" and gives Japan equality with the Western powers.

(1900) Paris International Exposition.

(1902) The Anglo-Japanese alliance is formed and Japan accelerates her military buildup.

(1903) The fifth Domestic Industrial Exposition is held in Osaka.

(1904–05) Japan's victory in the Russo-Japanese War establishes Japan as a regional superpower, but at massive human and financial cost.

(1904) The Louisiana Purchase Exhibition in St. Louis.

(1905) The Universal and International Exposition in Liège, Belgium.

(1907) The Tokyo Industrial Exhibition is held, continuing the tradition of the Domestic Industrial Expositions.

(1909) Completion of the Akasaka Detached Palace by Katayama Tokuma symbolizes Japanese mastery of Western architecture.

(1910) Japan annexes Korea. The Japan-Britain Exhibition is held in London.

(1912) Death of the Meiji Emperor.

W. G. Beasley, *The Rise of Modern Japan. Political, Economic, and Social Change since 1850* (New York: St. Martin's Press, 1995). A diachronic survey of Japan's interaction with the West from the Meiji Restoration through two world wars and her economic miracle of the 70s–80s. The story ends with 1994, before the current Asian economic crisis developed.

Richard Bowring and Peter Kornicki (eds), *The Cambridge Encyclopedia of Japan* (Cambridge: Cambridge University Press, 1993). A very useful source of information about Japan, profusely illustrated, and presented in a reader friendly manner.

Hugh Cortazzi, *The Japanese Achievement* (New York: St. Martin's Press, 1990). Records the history of Japan since the "beginning of recorded time," looking at political, economic, social, literary, and artistic aspects.

Joe Earle, *Japanese Art and Design* (London: Victoria and Albert Museum, 1986). A beautifully illustrated survey of the Toshiba Gallery at the Victoria and Albert Museum, with an especially good focus on textiles and ceramics.

Victor Harris, *Japanese Imperial Craftsmen: Meiji Art from the Khalili Collection* (London: British Museum Publications, 1994). This is the catalogue for an exhibition of selected works of art from the Khalili Collection which was on view at the British Museum in 1994.

William Hosley, *The Japan Idea: Art and Life in Victorian America* (Hartford: Wadsworth Atheneum, 1990). The catalogue for an exhibition held in 1990 at Hartford's Wadsworth Atheneum, which sheds light on just how pervasive and important the idea of Japan was to American society of the period. Of particular interest is the intersection of that craze with the women's suffrage movement and the startling impact on American culture.

Janet E. Hunter, *The Emergence of Modern Japan: An Introductory History Since 1853* (London and New York: Longman, 1991). Not really a history in the traditional sense of dates and events, but rather a study of political, social, and economic developments aimed at providing the Occidental reader with insight into the nature of Japan by challenging received wisdom's misconception about the monolithic nature of Japan life and society.

Oliver Impey and Malcolm Fairley (gen. eds.), *The Nasser D. Khalili Collection of Japanese Art*, volumes I–V (London: The Kibo Foundation, 1995). This multi-volume set contains essays by an international consortium of scholars and documents the objects, acquired up to 1995, in the Khalili Collection with color photographs and scholarly catalogue entries.

Oliver Impey and Malcolm Fairley, *Treasures of Imperial Japan: Ceramics from the Khalili Collection* (London, The Kibo Foundation, 1994). This is the exhibition catalogue for a selection of ceramics in the collection which was on view at the National Museum of Wales in Cardiff in the fall of 1994.

Marius B. Jansen, *Sakamoto Ryoma and the Meiji Restoration* (New York: Columbia University Press, 1994). The history of the Meiji Restoration told by focusing on the career of Sakamoto Ryoma, and to a lesser extent on that of his contemporary Nakaoka Shintaro, both of whom were murdered shortly after the shogun's resignation. Sakamoto's posthumous reputation as a cult hero of the period has not affected the author's incisive assessment of his role in the transition.

Marius B. Jansen and Gilbert Rozman (eds.), *Japan in Transition from Tokugawa to Meiji* (Princeton: Princeton University Press, 1988). A collection of seventeen specialized essays by leading scholars, divided into four topics for investigation which include administration, organizations (civil, military, religious, and commercial), cities and their populations, and rural economy and material conditions.

Julia Meech-Pekarik, *The World of the Meiji Print. Impressions of a New Civilization* (New York and Tokyo: Weatherhill, 1987). Dealing with a classification of objects which lie outside of the collecting scope of the Khalili Collection, this volume presents a view of Meiji society through the lens of the period's print makers, some of whose illustrations provide biting social commentary on the mores of both Japanese and foreigners alike.

Kazu Nishi and Kazuo Hozumi, *What is Japanese Achitecture? A Survey of Traditional Japanese Architecture* [Translated, adapted, and introduced by H. Mack Horton] (Tokyo, New York, and London: Kodansha International, 1983). A handy guide to traditional styles and architectural detail, often accompanied by line drawings, divided into ecclesiastical temples and shrines, residential and urban residences, castles and their towns, and edifices for entertainment both legitimate and otherwise.

Mavis Pilbeam, *Great Civilisations: Japan 5000 B.C. to Today* (New York: Franklin Watts, 1988). A colorfully illustrated era-by-era account of Japanese history, with helpful date charts and good index.

John Reeve, *Living Arts of Japan* (London: British Museum Publications, 1990). An excellent introduction to many aspects of Japanese culture (including the fine arts, calligraphy, martial arts, clothing, and food) attractively illustrated and linked, where possible, to objects in the collections of the British Museum.

J. Thomas Rimer, *A Reader's Guide to Japanese Literature* (Tokyo and New York: Kodansha International, 1980). Selects twenty classical works and an additional thirty modern works and provides a commentary for each. The classical works include *Kojiki* ["Record of Ancient Matters"], *The Tale of Ise*, *The Tale of Genji*, *The Tale of the Heike*, and *The Love Suicides at Amijima*. The modern works include *Kokoro* (Natsume Soseki), *Before the Dawn* (Shimazaki Toson), *Snow Country* (Kawabata Yasunari), *Silence* (Endo Shusaku), and *The Temple of the Golden Pavilion* (Mishima Yoshio).

Joan Stanley Baker, *Japanese Art* (London: Thames and Hudson, 1986). An introductory guide from prehistory to the present of many aspects of Japanese culture.

H. Paul Varley, *Japanese Culture* [Third edition] (Honolulu, University of Hawaii Press, 1984). A very convenient place to turn to first for authoritative but felicitously written discussions about Japanese cultural life, told in chronological fashion from Japan's early formative periods to the present. Religion, literature, fine and performing arts, architecture, and even the modern Japanese cinema are among the wealth of topics treated.

http://jin.jcic.or.jp/kidsweb/
This is the address for a brand new website set up by the Japan Center for Intercultural Communications on the Japan Information Network. It provides basic information on various aspects of the country for school children aged 10 to 14.

http://www.jnto.go.jp/
This is the address for the Japan National Tourist Organization (JNTO).

Cat. 108

Earthenware ceramic Bowl, 15.3 cm. in diameter, created between 1900 and 1910, signed with a gilt seal Yabu Meizan, the foot-rim impressed Meizan.

The extravagantly enameled and gilded Japanese earthenware called "Satsuma" captured the imagination of both European and American writers at the very start of the Meiji Era (1868–1912) and was perhaps the most extravagantly praised of all Japan's newly discovered arts and crafts. Combining infinitely painstaking craftsmanship with mysterious subject matter, "Satsuma" was among the most successful of Meiji-Era Japan's efforts to produce goods that appealed to the Western taste for the exotic.

Yabu Meizan (1853–1934) of Osaka was the most prolific of the many manufacturers of Satsuma ware and his family still own many of the medals that he won at exhibitions from 1885 until 1916 in cities as diverse as Kyoto, Paris, Chicago, Hanoi, St Louis, Portland, London, Osaka, and Semarang in Dutch Indonesia.

Cat. 211

Porcelain trumpet-shaped Vase, 42.5 cm. in
height, created between 1900 and 1910,
signed Makuzu Kozan.

Porcelain, a white-bodied ceramic ware fired
at a very high temperature and usually with
a transparent glaze, was first made in Japan
around 1600. After a period of decline in the
early 1800s, the porcelain industry revived in
the middle of the nineteenth century as it
rapidly came to terms with the high standards
demanded by the global market.
The subsequent porcelain boom was
spearheaded by Makuzu Kozan (1842–1916),
one of the greatest potters of the Meiji Era.
He took over the family business in 1860 at
the tender age of nineteen and in 1870
opened a workshop in Yokohama, which
was becoming a magnet for businessmen
and tourists from all over the world. Makuzu
Kozan continued to produce wares of the
highest quality in a very wide range of
designs right up until the end of the Meiji Era.

Cat. 314

Cloisonné enamel Vase, 35.3 cm. in height, created about 1910, signed with an engraved seal of Ando Jubei.

In cloisonné enameling, different areas of colored glass paste, separated from one another by thin strips of wire (*cloisons*) placed edgeways, are applied to a metal base and fired at a high temperature until the paste fuses. Although the technique had been known in China since the fourteenth century, it made little headway in Japan until about 1850, but already in the 1880s Japanese enamels were one of the wonders of the world, and by the beginning of the twentieth century they far outstripped anything that had been achieved before in the medium anywhere in the world. Another twenty years on, Japanese enameling was in decline, and today it would be impossible to reproduce the achievements of the great craftsmen whose works are shown in this exhibition. This vase was decorated using a technique in which the traditional dividing wires are either concealed or removed before the final polishing. This new technique enabled the artist to achieve an effect close to painting in his depiction of the distant snow-capped peak of Mount Fuji, rising above clouds beyond a lake fringed by pines and maples in rich autumnal colors. This particular vase was exhibited in the Japan- British Exhibition in London in 1910, the last of the great international exhibitions held during the Meiji Era.

Cat. 225

Cloisonné enamel Vase, 172 cm. in height,
created around 1893.

This massive cloisonné enamel vase originally
formed part of a three-piece garniture
made expressly for the World's
Columbian Exposition in
Chicago in 1893, the greatest
public event of the Gilded
Age and attended by more
than 27,000,000 visitors. In
the accompanying catalogue,
the vases of that garniture were
described as "the largest examples of cloisonné enamel ever
made." Although the name of the
actual artist is not preserved, the catalogue entry does credit Shin Shinwoda
(actually Shin Shioda), Special Counselor
for Arts of the Japanese Commission to
the World's Columbian Exposition, with
the conception of the design. The catalogue goes on to enumerate the other
artists, craftsmen, and skilled workers
who formed the wonderful consortium
of talents that ultimately created the
component elements of the garniture. The side of the vase selected
here for illustration depicts two
eagles, one perched on a
pine-branch, the second
below, on a rocky ledge
scattered with grasses, bamboo, and autumn
leaves. The neck is decorated with alternate
red and white bands of chrysanthemums and
paulownia, and the upper part with applied
stars. The sides of the vessel are fitted with
handles in the form of chrysanthemums from
which are suspended patterned swags of
imitation bunting. The base is adorned with
formal foliate and floral motifs. When displayed in Chicago, the vase was supported
by a carved wooden pedestal, contributing
to the impression of its colossal size; that
pedestal has not survived.

The motifs on the vase are polyvalent in
meaning. On the one hand, the two eagles
in their environment may represent autumn,
the corresponding scene on the reverse of
this vessel winter. On the other hand, the
eagles could be interpreted as emblems of
the United States of America, appropriate for
decorative motifs for the World's Columbian
Exposition, and reinforce the references on
the neck to the Stars and Stripes of the
American flag.

Cat. 174

Lacquer Vase, 65.8 cm. in height, created between 1880 and 1890, inscribed in gold *hiramaki-e*, a lacquer technique, made by Nagata Toratsume, produced by the Gyokkendo Company.

This vase is based on a Chinese bronze shape, with decoration in gold and silver lacquer, shell, ivory, and other materials. The large inset panels on each side depict scenes from Chinese and Japanese legend. On the side shown in this photograph the unruly Shinto creation deity Susano-o offers a jewel to his sister, the Sun-Goddess Amaterasu, from whom all the emperors of Japan were believed to be descended. Rays of the sun radiate from her head and the moon can be

seen behind the willow tree. A dragon, originally a Chinese imperial emblem but long ago appropriated by Japanese artists, peers round from behind her and egrets circle above. The smaller panel in the neck depicts cranes flying amid stylized clouds. Amaterasu was so shocked by Susano-o's violent deeds that she withdrew to a cave and could only be enticed out by an erotic dance. She at last emerged, and the world was restored to light. There followed a struggle between Amaterasu and the descendants of the banished Susano-o. At last the Sun Goddess sent her grandson Ninigi to rule over the land. Ninigi was the great-grandfather of Jinmu, Japan's first tenno or emperor, who is supposed to have

ruled from the year 660 B.C. Not long before the Meiji Restoration (1868), when Japan had been governed by military leaders for hundreds of years, several Japanese thinkers started to remind their countrymen of the emperor's direct descent from Amaterasu. Japanese people, especially independent-minded members of the warrior class, grew more and more concerned about their government's failure to take action against the threat of Western invasion, and their opposition found expression in emperor-centered nationalism. After the emperor's power had been restored, the Meiji leaders made Shinto the Japan's official religion and gave Amaterasu and her family a prominence they had never enjoyed before.

Cat. 187

One of a pair of Tusk-Vases in the form of an elephant, 90 x 38 cm., created about 1885, signed made by Kaneko.

The elephant itself is sculpted from wood, covered with the bright gold *kinji* lacquer beloved of Meiji-Era artists and inset with a pair of silver tusks. It rests on a separate black lacquer stand covered with figured silk on its upper surface. Its elaborate undercloth and trappings are encrusted with hardstones and silver, embellished with designs in cloisonné enamel. The highly ornate saddle, also in cloisonné enamel, is adorned with silver tassels so realistically rendered that they appear to sway gently as the pachyderm walks.

The saddle is decorated with a foliate stand on which rests a curved section of an ivory tusk, decorated with two separate scenes. One portrays the Chinese Emperor Genso and his concubine Yokihi playing a flute in an idyllic garden setting. The other depicts a hawk perched on a rock by a stream. This piece is one of a pair that had been separated for many years until they were brought together to form one of the highlights of the Khalili Japanese Collection.

▶
Cat. 377

A lacquer Cabinet presented as a gift to the future British King Edward VIII, 110 x 51.1 x 103 cm., created between 1904 and 1911 by Harui Komin.

This wonderful piece of furniture consists of two cupboards in diagonally opposite corners, each with a pair of doors hinged at the sides and with a central opening. To one side of each cupboard there are additional cupboards with sliding doors, drawers below, and staggered shelves formed by the tops of the cupboards.

The fronts of the cupboards, the sliding doors, and the drawer-fronts themselves are each decorated with the traditional Chinese scenes known as the "Eight Views of Xiao and Xiang" after the Xiang River and its tributary the Xiao which empty into Lake Dongting in Hunan Province. The interiors are separately decorated with varied scenes including fabulous beasts, floral motifs, and landscapes. The back of the cabinet is adorned with floral roundels, most of which contain a bird, insect, or animal appropriate to or

seasonal with the plant shown. So, for example, a squirrel is paired with a vine and hare with horsetail. A letter, recently discovered by chance among the papers in the archives of London's Victoria and Albert Museum, provides the background to the manufacture of this most resplendent example of the classical revival style of the late Meiji (1868–1912) and Taisho (1912–1926) Eras. Dated 12 April 1922 and mailed from Tokyo, the letter's author, Baron K. Sumitomo, explains how this cabinet was his commission to "Komin Harui" (putting the artist's name in the Western order with the family name last), whom he describes as the master overseeing the creation of relief lacquer wares, called *makie-shi* in Japanese. The Baron then enumerates the cast of tens who were occupied for seven years in the creation of this cabinet, four of which were laboriously spent on the laying of the relief gold lacquer. The present cabinet is the largest piece of lacquer known by Komin, an obscure figure who retired to Suma near Kobe in 1914 where, as a devout Buddhist, he continued to live and work in quiet isolation, despising both money and worldly honors.

When Prince Hirohito then visited Britain in 1921 in order to cement peace and goodwill between the two countries, he personally presented this cabinet to his royal counterpart, the Prince of Wales, later for a brief period King Edward VIII of Great Britain.

Cat. 1

A bronze Incense Burner, 280 x 130 cm.,
created in the 1870s, signed Kako, the
art-name of Suzuki Chokichi (1848–1919).

This massive bronze incense burner featuring
a large eagle as its finial is designed as a
bowl supported by three muscular demons
standing on a rockwork base. The demons
are characterized by ferocious expressions,
and one is horned. All are partially clothed
and each supports the bowl in a distinctive
way. One raises both arms, the second just
one arm and the third his head. Their eyes
and ear bangles are gilt. This remarkable
piece was doubtless created for a major
international exposition, which cannot now
be identified. In tracing its subsequent history
one can establish that it was acquired in
Europe before 1886, at which time it entered
a public collection in Germany. After a series
of vicissitudes, including its legal deaccession,
it passed into private hands. Its maker, Suzuki
Chokichi (1848–1919), who used the *go* or
art-name Kako, was one of the foremost
bronze-casters of the Meiji Era. Like many
of his contemporaries, he started his career
with a traditional training, came to prominence
during the 1870s and 1880s, ran a flourishing
business until the first decade of the twentieth
century and then died in relative obscurity
a few years after the Meiji Era came to a close
in 1912. Born in the western suburbs of
Tokyo, he was apprenticed to a workshop in
the city, learning his craft there for five years
until setting up on his own at the age of
seventeen. Among his greatest works are
vast bronze incense burners made for
international exhibitions in Vienna (1873),
Philadelphia (1876), and Paris (1878), a great
bronze lantern for the Yasukuni Shrine in Tokyo
(1880), a fountain for the second National
Industrial Exposition (1881), and an eagle
which won first prize at the Nuremberg
Metalwork Exhibition (1885). His most
famous piece is the set of twelve life-size
bronze falcons he exhibited at the Columbian
World's Fair in Chicago (1893). As well as
being a supremely skillful worker in bronze,
Chokichi was also an astute businessman. In
1874 he became director of the metalworking
department of a government-sponsored
export company, the Kiritsu Kosho Kaisha,
setting up his own firm after the company
folded in 1891. Chokichi was appointed
Teishitsu gigeiin ["Artist to the Imperial
Household"] in 1896.

Cat. 232

A colossal bronze Eagle, 235 cm. in height
with a wing span of 244 cm., created about
1890.

Suzuki Chokichi, the creator of the magnificent
incense burner which is also on view in this
exhibition, continued to excel in his craft
after the closing of the state-sponsored
Kiritsu Kosho Kaisha Company in 1891, for
which he served as director. By consensus
his most famous work, now in the Crafts
Gallery of the Tokyo National Museum of
Art, was a set of twelve metal falcons
commissioned by Hayashi Tadamasa and
exhibited at the World's Columbian
Exposition in Chicago in 1893.

Contemporary photographs of the entrance
to the Japanese section of the Fine Art Building
at the World's Columbian Exposition show,
in addition to the twelve falcons, a large
bronze eagle similar to this piece which may
also be the work of Chokichi or a follower.

Cat. 396

Bronze Plaque, 36 cm. in diameter, created about 1910, signed by Unno Shomin (1844–1915).

This plaque was made from carved and inlaid copper, the eyes of the figures inlaid with silver and with *shakudo* [gold-copper alloy] pupils, and set into a wooden frame. Unno Shomin, one of the greatest of all Meiji-Era metalworkers, specialized in a Japanese chiseling technique, *katakiri-bori*, that allows for variation in the width of the engraved line. This masterpiece, one of two such plaques by Shomin in the Khalili Collection, is really a painting in metal, with every natural, flowing detail of Kanzan and Jittoku's hair painstakingly delineated with countless strokes of the hammer on the chisel in place of the delicate, and a hundred times more rapid, touch of a Japanese brush on paper. Like many of the leading artists of the period, in 1896 Shomin was named *Teishitsu gigeiin* ["Artist to the Imperial Household"].

Appropriately for a work imitating the effects of ink-painting, a technique originally introduced to Japan from China, the subject matter depicts two legendary Chinese personalities, eccentric monks who lived during the Tang Dynasty (618–907) in the kitchen of a Buddhist monastery and conversed in their own private language. For this reason, both were considered mentally unbalanced. Kanzan is here shown reading a scroll to Jittoku, who is holding a broom.

Cat. 168

Silver Incense Burner in the form of an
elephant, 37.1 cm. in height, created about
1890, signed by Shoami Katsuyoshi
(1832–1908).

This incense burner is modeled as an
elaborately caparisoned elephant with a richly
embellished harness comprising a bejewelled
saddle-cloth adorned with masks of *shishi*,
mythical Chinese lions, and images of
minogame, long-tailed turtles emblematic
of long life. The saddle-cloth supports a
coiled dragon standing on swirling clouds
and holding a large rock-crystal ball. The
head-dress of the elephant is in the form
of a stepped pedestal which supports a
golden *ho-o* bird with spread wings.
Details of the caparison are inlaid in a
variety of disparate materials including
rock crystal, malachite, coral, tiger's eye,
agate, and nephrite.

This piece is replete with symbolic overtones
which provide a window onto the spiritual
landscape of the Japanese character at
the time of the Meiji Restoration
(1868). The white elephant possesses
great significance in Buddhism as
the preferred mount of Fugen, the
bodhisattva of wisdom. The white
elephant was also reported to be
one of the animals present at the
death and final enlightenment of
the Buddha. Its saddle is in the
form of a lotus which is not only a
symbol of rebirth but also
the throne for all holy
beings in Buddhism. The
dragon supports a crystal
ball which in popular
legend represents the jewel that
controls the tides. Furthermore, the
crystal ball, by virtue of its clarity and
brightness, represents the essence of the
Buddha's teaching. It metaphorically replaces
the bodhisattva who usually rides upon the
back of the white elephant.

The artist, Shoami Katsuyoshi, began to
study metalworking techniques at the age
of thirteen and was an accomplished
craftsman five years later. Like many of
his contemporaries, he was initially a
manufacturer of sword-fittings but with the
demise of the samurai class as a result of the
policies of the reforming Meiji government,
he was forced to adapt to changing conditions.
He redirected his talents and placed them
at the disposal of new styles and different
commissions in the early 1870s. So successful
was he in this transformation that he won
numerous prizes while exhibiting extensively
in local and international exhibitions.

Cat. 172

A bronze Group of Susano-o no Mikoto
receiving the sacred jewel, 99 x 80 cm.,
created after 1881, signed by Otake Norikuni
(b. 1852).

Susano-o, the "Impetuous Male Deity," is
shown wearing an ornately patterned coat
and voluminous trousers gathered below
the knee. Around his neck is a necklace of
magatama, curved beads, and tigers' claws.
The sea-god is wrapped in a windswept
coat hung with seaweed, spiked tassels, and
a dragon-fish. The baroque composition is
inhabited by a host of real and fabulous
creatures imparting a fantastic and ghoulish
feeling to the eerie scene, which is
described in great detail in an inscription
found on the underside of the base. That
inscription claims that Tomita Tetsunosuke
composed the text, the engraving of which
is the work of Katakura Akinori.

In this version of Japan's creation myth
Susano-o no Mikoto, in violation of his father's
wish that he rule the Seven Great Islands, opts
instead to rule the underworld. His father
consents. At that very moment, a god called
Haneakarutama no Mikoto offers Susano-o a
beautiful jewel called the *mizu-yasakani no
magatama*, which becomes one of Japan's
Three Sacred Treasures of Mirror, Sword, and
Jewel. Susano-o was so pleased with this gift
that he promptly traveled back to heaven
and presented the jewel to Amaterasu the
Sun-Goddess, who was also his sister. That
scene is depicted on a lacquer vase in this
exhibition, page 85, above.

Otake Norikuni was originally called Otake
Eijiro, and learned his craft from his like-
named father whom he succeeded in 1871.
He was a highly regarded artist in his lifetime and received many prestigious
commissions. A major exhibitor at both
domestic and international expositions,
he was also a gifted teacher and several
of his pupils went on to stellar careers
of their own.